Tarot for Teens

The Ultimate Tarot & Ritual Guide for Young Mystics

By: Jane Rivers

Copyright © 2021 by Jane Rivers

ALL RIGHTS RESERVED

No part of this book may be reproduced, stored in a retrieval system, or transmitted in any form or by any means, electronic, mechanical, photocopying, recording, scanning, or otherwise, without the prior written permission of the publisher.

Limit of Liability/Disclaimer of Warranty: the publisher and the author make no representations or warranties with respect to the accuracy or completeness of the contents of this work and specifically disclaim all warranties, including without limitation warranties of fitness for a particular purpose. No warranty may be created or extended by sales or promotional materials. The advice and strategies contained herein may not be suitable for every situation. This work is sold with the understanding that the publisher is not engaged in rendering medical, legal or other professional advice or services. If professional assistance is required, the services of a competent professional person should be sought. Neither the publisher nor the author shall be liable for damages arising herefrom. The fact that an individual, organization or website is referred to in this work as a citation and/or potential source of further information does not mean that the author or the publisher endorses the information the individuals, organization or website may provide or recommendations they/it may make. Further, readers should be aware that websites listed on this work may have changed or disappeared between when this work was written and when it is read.

CONTENTS

Introduction 1

Part 1: A Brief History of the Tarot 3

Part 2: The Tarot Workbook - Meanings 15

Part 3: The Best Tarot Spreads for Beginners! 107

Part 4: Tarot Magic! Manifestation and Growth Rituals with the Tarot 131

Part 5: Intuitive Tarot Reading 145

Part 6: Bringing in the Beings and Keeping It All in the Family 159

INTRODUCTION

The Tarot has a rich history throughout many continents. The last two generations in the West have enjoyed Tarot as a popular trend, but that which doesn't work will not stay around long. The longevity of the Tarot proves it's hardly a passing fancy.

The Tarot is much more than just a divination tool and a mystery shrouded in superstition and myth. It's just one tool that allows the user to tap into the secrets of nature that are no secret at all. We've been programmed to believe that it's dangerous or the work of some evil entity, when in reality it's as natural as breathing air.

The Tarot works on the basis of truth. If you ask, it shall be told without bias. That means the Tarot and the Universe, which is essentially what you're speaking to, has no care about personal feelings, political correctness, societal rules, or religious beliefs. It only tells the Truth. We'll go over all of these principles in an easy-to-understand manner and where appropriate in this guide.

What You'll Learn in This Guide

You'll learn what the Tarot really is and how it works. We unravel the mystery without ruining the magic. Acquire wisdom in simple terms while confidently practicing the art with a firm, well-rounded grasp of the history, meanings, and principles of the Tarot.

How to Prepare to Use This Guide

We thought we'd inform you from the beginning what tools you will need to begin the Tarot and list them here. One disclaimer: You don't need to use these tools each time. We're only guiding you here, so you don't have to follow any one tradition.

The Tarot is not associated with any religion although here, we decided that the simplest tools and Tarot rituals are from the Wiccan tradition. Yes, they are commonly called witches, but not all who practice Wicca identify with being a witch. Since the Tarot works in tandem with nature, the Wiccan and other Earth Magic based traditions seemed the most fitting.

Tools

1. **Your own Rider-Waite Tarot deck:** This is the clearest and easiest to follow deck and used traditionally for beginners. We will be using the symbolism for this deck in this guide.
2. **White candle:** If you can get a glass-enclosed seven-day novena candle, that would work better and be a lot safer, especially if you're not used to candle burning on an altar. A seven-day candle also works best for the Tarot rituals.
3. **A pack of white votive candles:** These are great for your Tarot spreads; always extinguish them after the reading.
4. **Sea salt and water**: This is to create protection over your reading and ritual space.
5. **An altar or altar space and altar cloth:** This can be made out of a cloth 9-inches by 9-inches square from any natural fabric like cotton, linen, or silk. If you aren't able to make one, they are sold online very cheaply and some are quite ornate.
6. **A Tarot pouch:** As with the altar cloth, you can purchase or make a Tarot pouch. This is to keep your Tarot cards in a sacred space out of the box.

Let's move on to the brief history of Tarot and give you some background to work with as a beginner.

PART 1: A BRIEF HISTORY OF THE TAROT

Though there are no records of exactly when the Tarot originated, we do know it was at least the 14th century, which tells us that there's something to it for sure. You'll read other accounts of the Tarot being representative of the Egyptian Book of the Dead and the Gods and Goddesses therein, but that and other theories dating back 5,000 years have been disproved after the interpretation of the ancient texts. However, divination in many forms does date back to the Babylonians, and Tarot is just a newer variation.

The traditional playing cards you may have seen your parents playing poker or a family card game with were the first real divination tools using cards in modern times. Later, there were additions made apart from the traditional court cards, and these appeared in Italy in the regions of Bologna, Milan, and Ferrara. They weren't called Tarot cards then, only the *Carte da Trionfi*.

In 1442, the royal family of Milan Visconti-Sforza had a set of Tarot cards painted for them; these cards were found some time later. There were court records before then in Ferrara as well, in the same year that mention only the *Carta da Trionfi*. These cards were known merely as a game called *Trumps*, or in Italian, *Tarocchi*. They were later reworked by those who knew and practiced the mysteries as a divination tool. We'll go more into that in the next section.

It wasn't until 1750 that evidence of actual methods, or as we call them today, Tarot Spreads, was found. In the 1800's a practicing mystic named Éliphas Lévi Zahed would later link the Tarot to the Jewish mysticism and the Tree of Life in the Kabbalah.

Whew! That is some history! From then on the cards were used as a form of official divination. Now, let's move more into the esoteric meaning before we go headlong into the exciting meanings, reading methods, and Tarot rituals.

What Tarot Really Is and How It Works

To understand how the Tarot works we must grasp the mechanics of the Universe. Before you start to feel overwhelmed, it helps to know that it's not complicated at all; but this is why we stated in the introduction that you shouldn't skip any of the information before you begin to work.

As we touched on earlier, the Tarot is used to interpret the Truth that the Universe wants to tell you. Whether it's answering a question or showing a possible outcome, the cards themselves are only a tool. They work on Universal synchronicity and, to some extent, what we call Law of Attraction today.

The truth is, if you take a handful of rocks, sticks, crystals, or any object and give each a meaning and then toss them on the altar or ground as you would Tarot or Runes or I Ching, you will get the Truth. The Universe doesn't care what you use because the cards have no special powers in and of themselves. You are the one training your personal Universe how you want an answer to show up.

When you go onto YouTube you see every type of divination possible so far. You have Tarot, Oracle, and even ink blot interpretation and energy paintings, as well as teacup, coffee grounds, and wax readings. The Tarot is no different.

There is one small caveat:

Any object or method has an energy and belief attached to it from the collective, meaning everyone, that has ever used it. You can tap into the energy each time you use the cards, and they will speak to you in the traditional way the Tarot books interpret the cards. In Tarot magic and ritual, you are also tapping into the collective and the results can be amazing.

Using Your Intuition:

The only more powerful thing is to use your own intuition. Just as you can create any form of divination you wish, you can use the cards intuitively, which we will teach you here. Intuition can't really be learned, but we will guide you with suggestions to get you started.

Your intuition can be developed with the Tarot and is used by many to do just that. You can then bring this natural skill that we all have dormant within us to assist you in making many decisions in life and to also help others. At some point, you may even begin to read for others after you've fine-tuned your skills and you're comfortable.

Tarot in Ritual

Tarot is used in ritual magic to manifest things you may want by using the Law of Attraction. They not only help your visualization, but the symbolism will help your subconscious kick in the power into the field of infinite possibility. The Universe works on symbols and emotions rather than words. The words in magic and rituals are only to conjure up the emotions you need. We'll go into best practices when we get to the basic Tarot ritual in this guide.

Myths About the Tarot

You're young and have so many people giving you advice and you'll find you have a lot of opinions about what you may be interested in. Tarot is no stranger to controversy in the West. The good news is the internet, when used properly for research, will save you from some of the myths and fear that others may place on the Tarot.

Tarot is Dangerous or Evil

We've already taught you that the cards have no power in and of themselves. They have no power to change your fate and they won't make something happen. The Universe has no interest in any religious or cultural beliefs or superstition; it's merely a machine in the case of divination. This is what we meant by the Tarot only tells the Truth by whatever means used and that's all.

So, in short, if you hear the Tarot is evil, dangerous, opens gateways to bad things and spirits, or is the work of some devilish entity connected to a religion or cultural belief, it's simply untrue.

Now, we're going to contradict ourselves here a little and tell you that there are best practices and protection which we created a section for. So, if the Tarot isn't evil why do we need that section?

The answer is simple. When you begin to open yourself up to the energies of the Universe, your spirit guides; angels, if you believe in that; and other beings can see your light.

You will automatically open up and begin to awaken. This is a beautiful thing, and you will grow beyond measure. Your wisdom and intuition will take you to great places, but the process must be respected, and you must have awareness that you are protected.

In that section, we will go into that further, but for now, the next Tarot myths!

The Tarot Tells the Future

This is not so. Yes, it's a divination tool, but it deals more with the fluid future. What does that mean? The future is always being formed. People do have a certain percentage destiny, but we understand what is going on according to the energies that we are in now.

The Tarot will only tell us what the probable outcome is based on what we are doing now. So, we should use the Tarot to take the wisdom of that information and make the best choices that we can.

The Death Card Means Certain Death!

This is a scary looking card, but remember it was illustrated at a time when people led less than fabulous lives. The plague was about, as well as the inquisition. There was quite a lot of death and destruction, which is why people looked for answers from divination.

The Death card predicts the death of the old to make room for the new. This could mean an ego death; when someone awakens, they start to realize some uncomfortable truths and they go through something called the Dark Night of the Soul. It's a time of wisdom and self-discovery. Sometimes it means the death of a relationship or friendship or even a career.

The important thing to remember about the Death card is it's an ending to something that wasn't the best for your growth.

The Tower Card Means Imminent Danger!

Like the Death card, the Tower is another ominous looking card. We will get into the meanings of all the Major Arcana in the workbook section but for now just the myths. The Tower can be the collapse of something and oftentimes it is the collapse of the old self.

It can be a sudden realization or even a sudden love affair! Its meaning, as with all the cards, depends very much on the subject and the context with the combination of the surrounding cards.

If You Throw Away Your Tarot Cards, It's Bad Luck

Okay, so if your Tarot looks like it's been through the worst and you can't see the images anymore, you can dispose of them without worry. Remember, it's what power you give to things that creates an issue.

The movies love to play on this with Tarot cards and Ouija boards. They'll portray all sorts of crazy things and you can just ignore it all. Paper and ink can't hurt you, curse you, or harm you in any way.

You Should be the Only Person to Touch or Use Your Cards

In this guide we do suggest that you keep your own personal deck to yourself and your own vibration. Why? Because they'll be easier to read when attuned only to you. We suggest that you have other decks you read for others for this reason as well, because for the beginner there can be carry over of energies and the reading can be muddled.

When you have more experience and can differentiate between your energy and that of another, you can feel free to mix it up. However, and this is very important to note: You are NOT in any way breaking any rule in reading for yourself and others with the same deck. This guide is for the beginner and this is why we make all the suggestions we do. We want your first experiences to be seamless.

Reversed Cards are Negative

  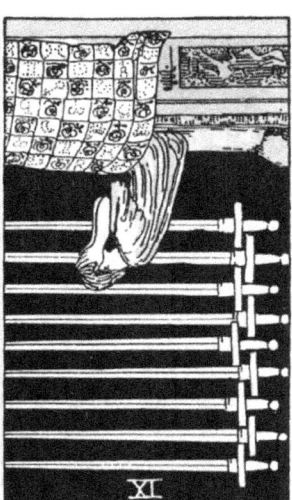

No, they are not always negative. As with all things Tarot, it is a matter of perspective and context. In fact, some cards you will want to see right side up because it means you've beat the negative connotation of the card. Yes, there are negative upright meanings too. You will learn all of that later.

These are the top myths that circulate out there in the esoteric and mainstream societies. A good rule of thumb is to look something up in a trusted resource and use your intuition that you will be developing here and elsewhere in your spiritual journey if you hear anything other than these few myths. Just keep in mind that if it sounds like it would make a good movie, it is probably not true.

Precautionary Measures for Safe, Enjoyable, and Effective Tarot Practices

Many times, we hear how dangerous spirituality is when in fact, it's no more so than any other belief that takes us into other realms of consciousness. This happens through prayer as much as it does through "magic" or "meditation" which IS a prayer.

You are either beseeching a deity or a spirit. Even if you are using the Universal energies or your higher self, you are still open to the 4th dimension. This is where mystics are taught everything both negative and positive hangs out.

One note on negative and positive energies: there is no real positive or negative. Energy cannot be harnessed like that. It is only balanced and imbalanced and that goes for what they call demonic energies and such. Once you understand this, you will never draw in or keep those energies around you.

If what we are taught over the ages is correct, then you draw in what you put out, even on a subconscious level. So, this is the basis of safe Tarot or spiritual practice and the perspective we will take going forward in this section.

A Few Rules of Thumb:

These are a guide only but taken from experience and for your peace of mind. It helps to note that most people who do simple protection rituals or none at all never experience anything bad.

Those who have, that tell the many tales of horror and then go join a religion to be saved from evil, are those who entered spiritual practices recklessly without a compass. Many more people have found great spiritual reward for their own lives and in helping heal others through their practice.

Regarding religions: Any religion, as we said earlier, opens your light to the 4th dimension. That's why we hear about possession and all the things people will tell you about spirituality. It is ALL spiritual and nothing besides taking care of yourself will protect you from any of it.

Tip One:

If you are afraid or apprehensive in any way using the Tarot, do more research and do not do it until you're ready.

Tip Two:

Make it all positive and sacred. You want positive vibes from your card deck—from what you keep them in to the area you use them in. Our suggestion is to have your own deck that you use for only yourself. Do not use them to read for someone else. No, this does not mean that if you do something bad will happen.

The purpose is to get used to sitting with your own energies and allow the Universal energies to flow much easier through to you. It is just cleaner for a beginner. When you are developing your intuition, you will be able to recognize your own energy signature without interference. Once you are adept at this, feel free to use your deck with others.

Create a nice cloth wrapping, pouch, or box to store and carry them in from a natural material so energies stay clean and flow easily. Next, create a small altar which you can buy on Amazon or build yourself from a natural material. You can buy them in portable form as well.

The whole point of this is to have a sacred space with your energy which in and of itself is protective. Yes, you are powerful and a part of the Divine creator and what you say goes. When you create a clean and clear space for your work, nothing negative is apt to follow. Watch your thoughts and intentions.

Tip Three:
For quick reads you can do any number of white or golden light meditations. Ten minutes is all you need. The point to mention is to keep your intention clear; to bring in the light and only beings of the highest realms to help you or your higher self. YouTube is full of some amazing ones and at the end of this book, we will give you some examples along with our recommended reading list.

For longer reading sessions try to take a ritual bath with Sandalwood or Frankincense and Myrrh oils. Those are the best ones we know of, but there are many out there so do some fun research of your own. There are some great ritual soaps out there too that you can use.

Sage the area with white sage. It gets really smokey so depending on how big your space is, you will want to experiment with about ¼ inch at a time and go from there.

Tip Four:

If you are completely new to spirituality, do not begin with any evocation to deities or spirits. Yes, maybe everyone has spirit guides, but they will be there anyway. They do not need evoking. Do not use any sigils or any high magic techniques for protection yet.

Take your time and use your higher self. As we said before; get to know your own energy and what *You* feel like. This is very important, because once you do this, you will be able to protect yourself even better in any circumstance because you'll be able to know the difference between your energy and someone or something else. Then, you can clearly intend it to be gone from your space.

Tip Five:

Learn to draw a boundary. Sea salt or table salt in some water. You can use rainwater; melted snow; water from a body of water like the ocean, lake, or creek; even ordinary tap water will do fine. In your sacred space or anywhere you wish to read for yourself, create a circle of salt or splash salted water around the area in a clockwise motion. When you are done you can take a broom and undo the circle in a counterclockwise motion.

If you are confident and without hesitation, you may simply imagine a circle of light around you. It is just as effective, but some feel more secure with a physical boundary that they can see. It is purely a matter of personal preference.

Tip Six:

Make certain that if you do evoke anyone, thank them and dismiss them to go where they came from in a loving and polite manner with gratitude. Then remove the circle.

These are the best six protection tips that you will ever need. In fact, most people use Tarot cards without any form of official, ritual protection. The reason why they have no issues is because they are not worried or thinking about spiritual danger. The law of attraction plays out in everything. We included protection tips to make the beginner or anyone who has already been bombarded by negativity about Tarot feel a lot safer.

PART 2: THE TAROT WORKBOOK - MEANINGS

Welcome to the Tarot workbook. We strongly suggest you go back and read section one thoroughly because we want you to have the best experience possible on your young and curious Tarot journey.

In this section, you'll find the meanings of the cards as they cover each section of life that you or someone you're reading for are likely to ask about. Each of the Major Arcana will talk more about the sections of life.

The Minor Arcana meanings are set in a story tone following the normal circumstances in life. This helps you to see the way the Tarot works and trains your mind from the very beginning to see them as the story of life.

An Easy Guide to the Major Arcana and Their Relation to Big Life Circumstances

Tarot Card Quick Reference Guide

22 Major Arcana in Order

Fool

This may denote a person that is not bothered about romantic encounters. This person is independent and free. In the case of someone wanting a relationship it may denote the type of person they need in their life; whether they know it or not, they are not suited for traditional relationships.

If they are already in a relationship, they may want to think about putting some playfulness in the mix. In some cases, this could denote a younger person, at least mentally, and/or a virgin.

In marriage it may denote the same as romance if already united with someone. Unions can be of any kind, not just marriage. The union may take on a playful tone with great adventure within it.

If it is reversed, then as in all the cards, it is the opposite and may need some fun infusion. This is also a very creative relationship.

In the case of a career, the person needs to work for themselves. This is not necessarily the high stress entrepreneur though. The fool is more of a freelancer that is more interested in working their own schedule and not so much networking to make "the big deal." This person would never be truly happy or thrive in a corporate environment.

Unless coupled with cards representing high compatibility, a business partnership is also not their ideal.

This person should be warned against frivolity in spending. However, careful investing could bode well for the Fool. As always, look at the surrounding cards to make that determination. Is there the Nine of Cups or Wheel of Fortune with the Ten of Pentacles?

You will get used to the card meanings as you learn them so do not sweat it right now, just practice. Creating budgets is not the strong suit of this character but if you make it fun, he can do it! And if you lock a certain amount of money away where it cannot touch, better yet.

The thing to remember about the Fool is he is not mindful because he has supreme trust in the Universe. This attitude can bring both positive and negative results to the Fool. The key is balancing diet and outlook for the Fool in health.

For the Fool and spiritual growth, he is always seeking and searching like a child so he's not showing signs of stagnation unless he's reversed. If you don't read reversals, then look at the surrounding cards and determine where the person is on their spiritual pathway.

Magician

The Magician is an interesting guy when it comes to romance. As a person he can be, in both a good and bad way, a manipulator. If you think he is representing a person, instead of doing the common and less accurate process of guessing an astrological sun sign, look at the characteristics in and of themselves.

What would the Magician be like to meet? Looking at the surrounding cards, ask yourself, "Would you date this person?" The Magician, when not a person in your reading, can represent a fiery, passionate romance on the horizon or an uptick in activity for an existing one. If it shows up with darker cards such as the Devil it may mean the querent must watch their back.

For marriages and partnerships of every kind the Magician, unless negatively placed, portends good things within an existing relationship. However, it could also mean whether unified or not, if you cannot have a relationship the way you want it you won't want it at all.

Career for the Magician is something toward entrepreneurship because of the fire and go-getter energy. The Magician is a self-starter with a natural leadership quality and is more mental than physical; that means success in endeavors like that are good for the person if the other cards indicate it.

The Magician can mean money from projects in chunks. If with the Four of Wands that is true for sure. They make a lot of money over time on a "by-project" basis. The financial status of the Magician is always good, but erratic.

If the person develops a freelance or entrepreneurial attitude about money, they'll be fine. The reversed card is a loss to erratic behavior with money but is typically temporary caused largely by their own attitude and actions.

A 'yes' is typical for the upright Magician but overturned or with negative cards means that it is going to be a delay the querent won't like. Sometimes, if you get confusing cards with it then it may mean that the decision is completely up to the querent.

The Magician is the great manifester and most of the destiny is in the Magician's hands.

Spiritual growth for the Magician is swift and confident. He or she can find the inner and outer guidance needed to grow on their own. If it is reversed, then they're hindering themselves.

High Priestess

The High Priestess does not typically look for a relationship actively. If it is offered, she will sit and assess the situation before deciding. She is typically too busy to think about love even when she's in a relationship; she's a go with the flow type of divine feminine energy.

This is a sacred marriage. It also may denote a handfasting done by some Earth religions which binds the couple for one year and one day, or three, seven or nine years. This is for the spiritual reassessment of the relationship for better planning and less drama like traditional ceremonies.

It does not mean that this will take place—it just means you are both out of the norm, or your partner is or will be. If with cards such as the Nine of Pentacles or Queen of Swords, you may not be bothered about a romantic union.

This person is made for a spiritual career. Or they may find a way to survive without having one as in an ashram or going off-grid in order to be a spiritual person. Some careers they may fall into are in the realm of spiritual teacher, healer, Tarot reader, and psychic medium.

Finances for the High Priestess, depending on the surrounding cards, can come from an inheritance, a partner, or spiritual work. It is also a bit erratic like the Magician because the High Priestess energy is a go with the flow, heavy manifestation energy. These energies are truly the successful but faithful in the Universal provision types. Use your intuition as to what you should invest in and when.

The High Priestess is a maybe answer, rather than a yes or no in most circumstances. Here is the difference: If it's surrounded by awesome, happy cards then it's a yes, but the answer may come in a way you least expect because the Universe wants to teach you something and deliver a surprise.

If it is surrounded by negatively oriented cards or reversed, it's most likely a No—BUT you may get what you need rather than what you want or better than you wanted. Have faith in the Universe!

This is a wonderful card for spiritual growth; simply put for beginners. Upright, on the right track, reversed or surrounded by not so good cards, it's stagnated. Ask questions of the High Priestess with the clarification cards and find out what you can do to strengthen your spiritual growth.

Empress

The Empress is fertile and loving. Regardless of gender, the person is full of creativity and so must be their partner. Depending on the surrounding cards, the Empress may portend a time of rest and reflection away from a relationship.

If it's surrounded by the Nine of Pentacles or Queen of Swords, then this could be the case. If it's near the Lovers or the Wheel of Fortune, then a choice between two suitors may be on the horizon.

If in Union, the person may be pregnant or their partner. One partner may have come into or needs to come into their receptive power for example, under or over giving. Not being able to receive. Look at the surrounding cards. The Nine of Wands or Temperance can be good indicators that can mean an imbalance. A comforting partner to marry is also indicated.

The career for the Empress can be anything from spiritual to homemaker, a counselor for those having relationship issues, a teacher of small children and more. She's empathetic and versatile. Look at the surrounding cards for the types of careers. It can also indicate a stall or temporary layoff from a job.

Finances may come in a steady flow if the energy of the person stays emotionally balanced. The source of the finances can be from a home based or agricultural job, freelancer position, or even a home teacher or schoolteacher. The Empress energy is also great for traveling jobs. This energy can be happy in any free or creative environment but not great in corporate.

This card is much like the High Priestess in that you really need to look at the surrounding cards. The Empress is an energy that is very fluid, so take it as a maybe until you analyze the surrounding cards.

The Empress is in touch with her emotions and her psychic intuition. If reversed, she needs chakra balance somewhere and the intuition to be unblocked. If it is upright, look to other cards to see where strengthening is needed.

Emperor

The Emperor is a domineering masculine energy. He can be possessive and maybe abusive. The surrounding cards will tell you.

In a union, the surrounding cards will tell you exactly how the Emperor's energy will behave and what to expect. As we mentioned, in romance this energy can go one way or the other quite abruptly. They can be a prince, or a nightmare and you will want to know.

A suggestion we can give you from experience is to do an extra spread to see your weaknesses in personality and see how it will interact with Emperor energy. You will want to work on yourself to get the best out of this type of personality or get away from it immediately.

A career for the Emperor can be anything from management to military as well as any leadership position which is typically higher ranking. This energy works above others or they own their own businesses and are best working alone.

Finances are good when this card shows up with positive cards. You can't predict with just one card on the Emperor. This energy could be the person stopping you from getting some form of financing. It can also mean an inheritance from an older man or what they call a sugar daddy or mama because gender doesn't always count; it's an energy.

This is a caretaker but sometimes with a price. If no one is attached to your finances, it will come in large chunks as an entrepreneur or in a steady flow from investments or corporate positions.

For a yes or no answer, look at the clarification cards. The Emperor on his own can be taken as a yes on simple questions. We would use at least one clarifier with this energy to confirm because there could be hidden energies.

Hierophant

Typically, the Hierophant is associated with marriage. Depending on the surrounding cards, you can tell if the relationship is going nowhere and being stopped by the conventions in the world and society, or if the marriage is going to take place.

Use clarifying cards to determine if the querent can do anything about the issue or if it's out of their hands. If it sits with another Major Arcana that is negatively oriented, you don't need to go any further to clarify because the Major Arcana are karmic and need no further clarification. Take the answer as it is for now, a probable no. If the other cards are positive, then it's probably a go but with some delays. In this case, you can use clarification cards to find more information about steps going forward.

Career and finance with this energy can mean the same as relationships. It's the stuffy sort of card in the deck. A strict set of rules about commitments are at play here. Look at the surrounding cards to determine if the person is liable to spend too much or hang on too tightly. Is the Fool or the Four of Pentacles nearby? This may denote extreme.

The career can be in government, clergy, or any high-ranking sort of religious or spiritual position such as priest or guru.

Lovers

The Lovers are often limited by the definition of choice between two people or meeting a potential partner. The lovers are more about choice in a relationship or any subject. The choice can be two pathways or whether to have one at all. The choice is not always just between a finite number like two. It can be a choice whether to take on a situation or wait it out.

In a union, you may be experiencing a lull in passion or a spark depending on the surrounding cards.

In the career position there can be several offers and, if paired with the Two of Cups or the Page of Pentacles, an introduction between you and a potential business partner could be on the horizon. For finances this may mean a choice of whether to invest or not.

For a yes or no question, the Lovers being a card of duality will need a clarifying card or two to determine the answer.

The spiritual meaning is the merging of the two sides of the self and a full integration of the universal forces within.

Chariot

You feel whirlwind in the area of romance. You don't feel comfortable at all and your interactions can be very awkward. There's a reason and the answer is in the clarifying cards. The Chariot is not one of the cards that can be used alone as its energy is chaotic.

The person you are interested in may be alluding you by acting strangely in your presence. If you're looking with no one in sight yet, then it's time to calm yourself and check if you're acting too desperately. If you're in a union with someone, there's something fabulous about to happen as a breath of fresh air is breathed into an existing relationship.

Career and finances can be erratic too. This card points to anxiety in decisions. If you're looking for a promotion or a new job, take some time out and reassess the situation and use clarifiers to determine the underlying issue.

This is another card that should have at least one clarifier in a yes or no question and should not be used on its own because its nature is chaotic.

Strength

The Strength in both love and unions is a good card. It only denotes the types of issues that take you from strength to strength in your relationships. If you're single, you may have to work on self-esteem issues or just simply your inner strength before taking on a healthy relationship. Don't get involved until those issues are resolved within so you can greet a new partner as a whole and healed individual.

In unions, you may be the one who tames certain elements of your partner or it could be them doing this for you.

In careers and finance this can mean a promotion or a pay raise for work well done. There are people on the way that resonate with strong energy and may headhunt you away from a current position. You are also great for entrepreneurial or freelance work as a business owner.

A yes is typically the answer for a yes and no question but with some delays that tend to be inner work needed. Use a clarifier to determine what that is.

Spiritual growth is intense with this card and may include an awakening, especially if you think you have already done it!

Hermit

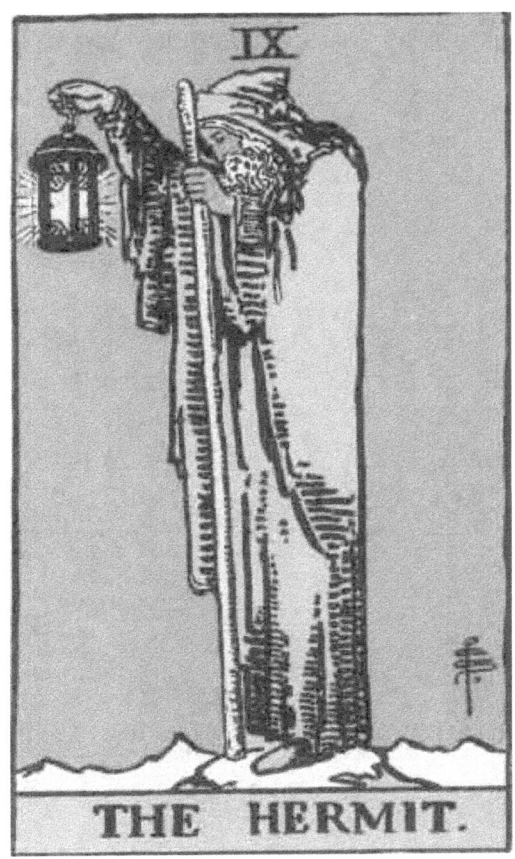

A new relationship is not suggested. Inner work is needed, and you still may run into lovers from the past to work on the karma you have had together briefly and bring it to a close. Some healing time is suggested.

In unions you may actually have some time apart. Not so much a formal separation as some time to yourself to be you without the relationship pressures. You will rejoin your partner renewed.

Careers and finances are about to change. Something is brewing behind the scenes and your intuition has been telling you this. Draw a few clarifiers to see what the issue is and how you can handle it.

In a yes or no, it is a maybe until you pull clarifiers to find out.

The spiritual growth meaning means that you are heading into the dark night of the soul or coming out of it. This happens because an awakening is taking place. We have many throughout our lives and this portends another soon.

Wheel of Fortune

Good or bad luck is the basis of the card in the popular definition, but it is so much more. In love, career, finance, or any question, this card is the most chaotic and must be clarified to find out what side of the Wheel is going to land on top. Which way will the Wheel turn? Ask the question with intention again and ask the Universe to convey what the outlying issues are that you are not aware of.

A word of warning here. The Universe uses cards like High Priestess and the Wheel of Fortune to dance around the occulted things in our life. You may not get a straight answer. A yes or no will need some serious clarification.

Justice

The Justice card in love can speak of karmic relationships. You may be experiencing painful or confusing issues in your romance or union and this means there is karma to work out together. Whether the relationship will last will be determined by the surrounding cards.

Career and finances can take a karmic twist as well with a sudden shift in status for good or for bad. Check the surrounding cards for the details. For example, if it is near the Page of Pentacles, or Nine or Ten of Pentacles or Cups, then you may have some good news. If the Devil, Four of Pentacles, or Nine of Wands shows up there, it may be an issue.

Yes or no is not possible with this card without a clarifier or two.

The spiritual lesson is purely karmic. Look at the chaos in your life right now or anything that you cannot seem to beat and pull cards in a separate reading with the Justice card in the middle to understand what you need to work on.

Hanged Man

To wait is to be rewarded with the best relationship of your life if you can prove to the Universe that you can work on yourself and change your perspective. Your vibration is almost there, and you want to raise it to draw in the best possible partner.

In unions you may have to learn to view your partner differently. The Major Arcana denote a fated situation. Is this a karmic relationship that you'll have to work through? Look at the surrounding cards to bring clarity.

In career and finances, advancement depends on your relationship to money. This one thing will give a life-changing boost to your career and life.

The spiritual lessons follow the same vein. It's time to work on perspective; and before you deal with the outside, practical world, you must change the way you view yourself and then the world. Everything else follows naturally when you master this.

Death

The most dreaded card in the deck and without good reason. The Death card is the most liberating card in the deck even though with it sometimes comes pain but oftentimes it brings relief. For good or for bad, the surrounding cards will tell.

Did you lose something you never really wanted or something you feel you could never replace? Have you broken up with a loved one? The Death card tells you that even though you may still pine for that loved one, there is better on the horizon. In a union there could be a resurgence in your relationship or a divorce. You must look at the surrounding cards.

Career and finance are a lull, layoff, or firing but for something better. In finance the stocks may take a plunge but do not sell just yet; it will all be resurrected!

Yes and no questions are relative here because it can be an ending of a good or bad result—clarifiers are needed.

The spiritual lesson here is the acceptance of change and letting go of the old to usher in the new. If you do not, you could be missing an incredible opportunity.

Temperance

The balance between romantic forces that may be quite incompatible. In romance or unions, there is an incompatibility that needs attention. You cannot do it alone and you shouldn't force something the Universe is trying to work on with you. Step aside and, like the Death card, accept what is and what will be. The issue may be that your partner may not be cooperating.

Career and finance follow the same premise for any situation. This is something happening around you that you want to control and that may prove futile. Ask the cards if there is anything you can do and if the answer is no, stand back and let fate fix it for you.

This is also the spiritual lesson of the Death card to learn to surrender.

Devil

The Devil is most associated with addiction and while that may be true, it is not just substance abuse. In love, it could be someone you are comfortable with and find it hard to let go.

You may make some excuse for their behavior or you are pining for someone that is not into you. If you are single you may be addicted to attracting people that are no good for you. In a union you may be the over giver or put up with some form of abuse.

Career and finance: This card will bring a lot of bondage in the same ways it does with any question. There is an unhealthy attachment to a job situation that is no good for you. Or an attitude or behavior pattern that is not in your best interest. Finances are stifled and the surrounding cards will illuminate the cause.

In a yes or no question it typically is a no but do clarify because if it means you will soon be released from this bondage, then you will be happier.

The spiritual lesson here is about why you think you need to be attached to unhealthy things. Place the Devil card in the middle and do another spread asking that question.

Tower

The Tower is one of the most terrifying cards in the deck next to the Death and Devil, and that fear is unnecessary. The Tower can portend a lot of upheaval that is unexpected and sudden. However, no matter what the situation is, it's the same message in love, career, finance, and spiritual lessons.

The Tower tells us that what Death, Temperance, the Wheel of Fortune and the Devil experiences were not able to purify and stabilize. That will be taken care of by the Tower. Once the Tower is involved, there is nothing you can do and nor should you. There is a new horizon after the storm.

If it shows up with the ten of swords, then that horizon is coming sooner than later. In a yes or no question, it is typically a no, but of course this is a chaos card and needs several clarifiers.

The spiritual lesson is that of surrender and perspective to change things by listening to the lesson of the other four chaos cards mentioned before the Tower must step in.

Place the Tower card in the middle of the spread and do a fresh card pull on what you can do to prevent further trauma.

Star

The Star is the beacon of hope in any situation, whether love, career, finance or spiritual lesson. The Star brings a fresh opportunity after the dark night of the soul and the drama that the last 5 cards mentioned here has brought in any situation, again, whether it be love, career, finance or spiritual lesson.

A resounding yes in a yes or no question is there for your taking—you've earned it!

Moon

The Moon is the next card after the reward of the Star for the past dark night of the soul. The Moon acts on its own in your life and in the area of romance and union; there is something going on in your subconscious or in your conscious mind causing fear and paranoia that is either necessary or unnecessary.

The surrounding cards and clarifiers will tell you how real the fear is. We suggest both a fresh spread with the Moon card as the middle card and pull clarifiers until you are clear.

Not getting to the bottom of the subconscious in this case will cause havoc to return and another dark night of the soul to reemerge. The Moon portends self-sabotage.

The spiritual lesson of the moon is to do the shadow work and release the spiritual blocks that are preventing you from seeing clearly and moving forward.

Sun

The Sun is right there with the Star in the love situation, though it can mean a lackluster feeling in the relationship if surrounding cards indicate it. Otherwise, a new flirtation can begin.

The Sun does not necessarily denote a serious relationship. It's more like the beginning of a fertile period. But in union, it may denote marriage. Look for the Hierophant and/or the Four of Wands and Ten of Cups and/or Pentacles.

Career or finances: You may feel like a career change, and finances may just not be what you want or deserve, but hope is on the horizon.

It's a yes in a yes or no reading and like the Star, no clarifiers are necessary. The spiritual lesson is to be grateful for what you have, to gain more of what you want.

Judgment

Judgment is the time of great karmic reckoning. It's similar to the Justice card but with the difference being that it's for your benefit. This means you are paid what you are owed in any situation. There may still be a sacrifice, but it is one you will not be unhappy about.

It is still considered a chaos card so a yes or no has to be determined with the clarifiers.

The spiritual lesson here is also one of accepting what you had to give up getting the karma you earned in a positive way. Be grateful and willing to receive and not repeat the same past mistakes.

World

The World in love affairs and unions, depending on the surrounding cards, will tell you if you will be satisfied in your relationship. Oftentimes, you will feel as if everyone else has what you want and you won't know how to get it. If the card is surrounded by more positive cards like the Ten of Cups, Nine of Cups, or Ace of Cups, it is satisfactory.

This card is the same in love, career, finance, and spiritual lessons. It's traditionally a yes in a yes or no question. The spiritual lesson is one of gratitude and assessment of what you have and the action to make it work. Mostly, it is patience at its core.

An Easy Guide to the Minor Arcana and Their Relation to Everyday Life and more Controllable Circumstances

How to Read the Minor Arcana

The Minor Arcana addresses the mundane, everyday affairs in life that we feel, act on, think about, and create out of the fated situations and life cycles the Major Arcana will present to us and take us through.

So, the simplest way to remember how to perceive the cards is like we describe here. The Major Arcana are the major life events for everyone from birth which the Fool represents as card zero and the World which is the completion of the life cycle.

The Minor Arcana are the everyday events that help or hinder as you travel through the fated life experiences. It is that simple. The reason why we did not split the meanings up into definitive categories, yet covered the most common ones, is because life is not neatly packaged into categories. Many circumstances will influence these 'categories' and will homogenize them.

Reading the Minor Arcana is simple because their meanings are simple. Knowing the basics of the suits will help you to grasp the meanings of the individual cards so you can create a fluid story throughout your spread.

The Cups are emotions that may come up in thoughts you did not know you were having in the subconscious. The Wands and Swords, as you will find out as you explore the Tarot, are interchanged depending on the author. Some have the Wands as action and the Swords as thought and some are vice versa. As you use the Tarot you can choose the meaning in your particular deck, or use them enough to get intuitive about it and determine the meaning that way.

The important thing to understand as a beginner is, you can never use them or interpret them incorrectly.

A Note on Reversals

We do not really include a full definition on reversals for the same reason why we do not place them in neat little categories. Think about it. What is negative and positive is relative to each person, so why throw their experience in a box, lock it up, and throw away the key? A good rule of thumb for a beginner is if it is reversed, it's the opposite of the upright position. Develop your intuition and you will never have to be concerned about reading them in reverse again.

The Meanings are Contingent on the Surrounding Cards

The meanings that you will see here are going to potentially represent different things. For Example: Ace of Cups could mean a new relationship, a flirtation, a marriage, or a dried-up, lax relationship, etc. Okay, so which is it? Look at the surrounding cards. What is their dignity? Are they positively or negatively oriented? Do they point toward or away from a relationship or good or bad feelings? If you keep in mind that it's a story, you can't go wrong. Never look at the cards as singular.

The Minor Arcana

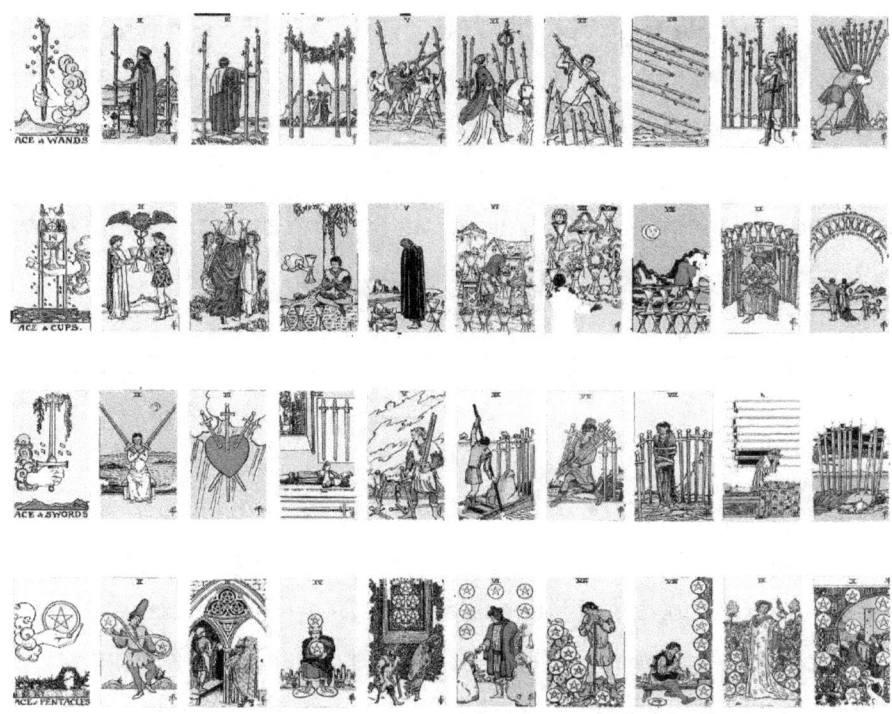

Minor Arcana

Ace of Cups

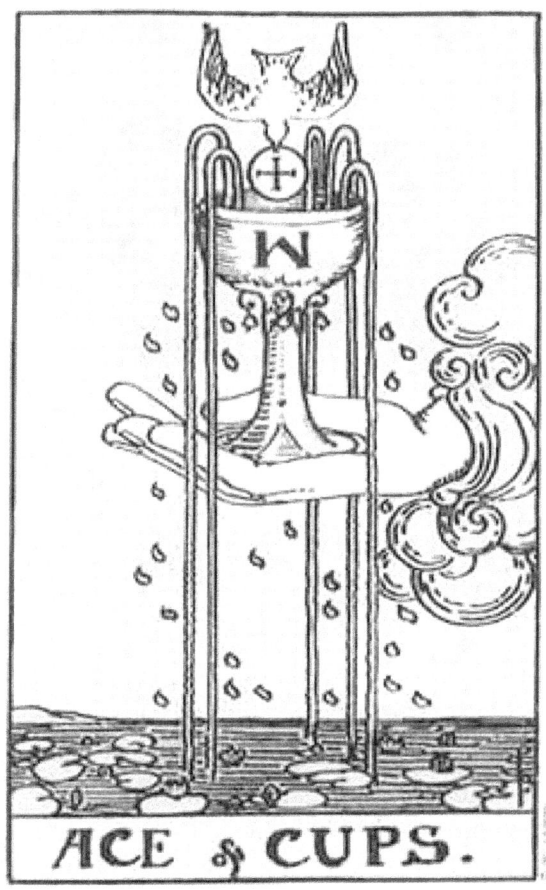

The pinnacle of emotion. What you have planted in your heart has turned up in the Universe and now you're seeing the results. You may have a new love affair coming toward you; are you ready? The seed to a new idea is showing a pathway to success. New beginnings in any relationship, new or existing. Get ready to be celebrated for what you do for a living or to help others. This is a communal card. Whether it is you and one other, or a group, it's about love in all its forms.

Two of Cups

Mutual attraction. A new partnership is offered in love or friendship. A new marriage proposal if other cards support it. Two people who are compatible. This can be platonic or not. In business, the perfect alchemy between two business partners is abundant.

Three of Cups

Celebration with friends. Balanced emotions. A new group direction is forming. Fruits of your labor through group effort are favorable. Make sure not to overindulge in drink.

Four of Cups

Boredom. Dwelling on past mistakes makes you leery of taking chances in the future. A purposeful turning away from the offers given.

Five of Cups

Self-pity. Really being a martyr emotionally. Emotional wreck from over exaggerated sense of loss that is unnecessary at this time. You turn from what you have with no regard for gratitude and miss the opportunities because you are still mourning the loss of the old.

Six of Cups

An old friend or lover appears from the past and warm exchanges abound. Sentimentality over things gone by. A peaceful dwelling on the sweet moments left. A reminder of the past. Acting from memories and not the present. Help comes from past friends.

Seven of Cups

Too many choices. How many are fantasy? How many can you reach? Do you want any of them and why? When you answer these questions, you'll be balanced enough to see clearly and choose correctly for yourself.

Eight of Cups

Walking away. Cutting cords. Abandoning that which does not work for that which does. You are asked to walk away into an unknown future with faith and resolve. Don't look back. Clean your feet at the door and lock it behind you, never to return. Sound scary? Then you're on the right track. Keep going!

Nine of Cups

You are working toward self-satisfaction. Is that what really satisfies you? Are you willing to do for others too, or have you abandoned all others for the self? Have an expression of gratitude for what you already have in order to gain more. Do something meaningful for deeper satisfaction that is lasting. Wish fulfillment.

Ten of Cups

Emotional completion that creates inner bliss. Family is together. Marriage if other cards support it. Kids if other cards support it. A possible new home in your chosen power place. Attainment of that which was sought after.

Page of Cups

A young lover. An innocent heart. Pregnancy if other cards support it. A stranger that comes bearing an opportunity for love and/or abundance.

King of Cups

A dreamy masculine energy in touch with his emotions. One who acknowledges the feelings of others and can draw them out gently. He makes you feel safe to express your heart. Most times loyal unless out of balance.

Queen of Cups

The caretaker. She can be an over-giver when she is out of balance. Nurturing when in balance. Intuitive and highly-sensitive. An empath.

Ace of Wands

New ideas await you! They are pouring in exponentially and you can hardly keep up with the opportunities. Grab the wand of opportunity with enthusiasm according to the surrounding cards. Your ideas are finally coming to fruition or a brand-new idea or opportunity is being handed to you—right now. The Wands are swift unless reversed.

Two of Wands

Okay, you can contemplate, but not too long. Do not turn contemplation into procrastination if reversed. What is your life's direction? What direction would be suited to your passion?

This is the question posed by this card. Apply it to anything you are asking about. Answer those questions and study the surrounding cards to find the hidden influences as to what may be causing either the procrastination or the contemplation.

Three of Wands

The rewards of your efforts are paying off! Congrats! The work you put in alone and typically with threes when with others, is paying off. Now there's room for a little celebration and then collaboration. This is the pause before new work begins for the real stability in the Four of Wands.

Four of Wands

The Four of Wands is the contemplation, planting of the seeds of stability. This card is still ripe for celebration as in the Three of Wands. This is because the Four is built upon the work of the Three of Wands.

You are safe here; this is what you call your home in your subjective experience. Home is different to different people. From a brick and sticks home to a hotel room while traveling the world. Either way, you have built this. Be proud of yourself but don't sit on your butt for too long. There is change coming in the Five of Wands!

Five of Wands

Now that you are bigger than life—in your subjective experience—and you have built your stability and what you'll call home, you have competition. This does not have to be fierce like the Seven of Wands. No, it can be playful and slightly envious type of people may be watching you or you may be watching them! If it's you then learn from them instead of wasting precious creative time worrying that they'll beat you!

Six of Wands

Victory! OK, so you have gotten through the first few wand card experiences and you've finally hit the jackpot! Make sure you are taking time to pop the cork on the magnum of champagne and enjoy your success. This time, you can take a bigger, longer hiatus from what you are doing without worry of the loss of business.

Seven of Wands

The Six of Wands has got you riding into town on your horse with a wreath hung upon your victory wand. People are noting you and that can make you feel on guard and defensive. Well, that means there are also jealous people because you are awesome! Take it in stride and do not let it get you down because most of it is an illusion, no one can really touch you.

Eight of Wands

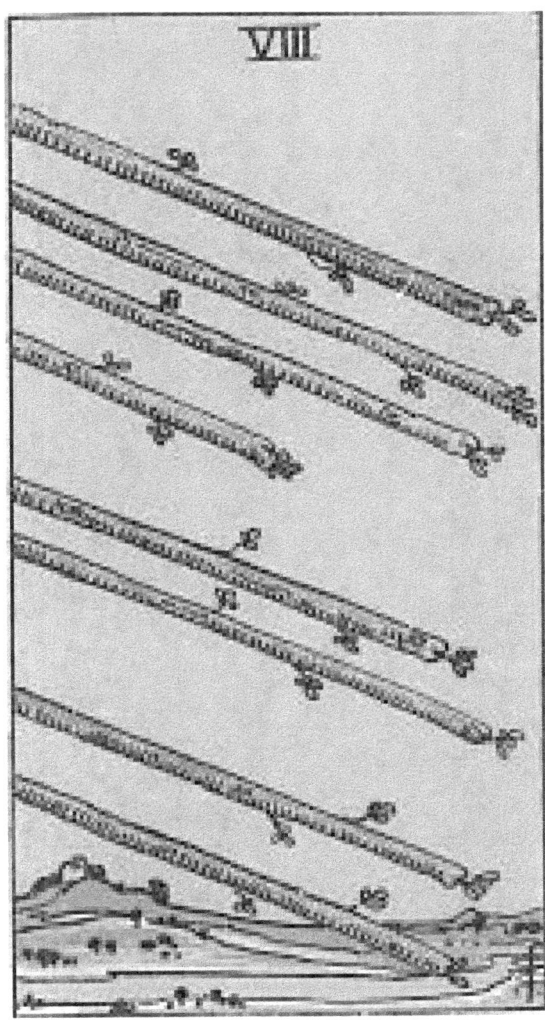

Communication is coming to you quickly. Be ready as they hold much opportunity. Make sure you do not act in haste and weigh out what you need to choose and do. Mistakes can be made that will cost you your victory and hard work. Study surrounding cards for the opportunities and pitfalls.

Nine of Wands

You may be falling into a feeling of being attacked or ambushed any moment. This can be illusory or real depending on the surrounding cards. Look at how many Cups there are reversed or negatively oriented. The Nine of Wands also portends the end of a cycle and this can bring on stress that can be unnecessary. Find balance.

Ten of Wands

You may not have looked deep enough into why you are still in the Nine of Wands energy and now you're taxed beyond what you feel you can do. Ask yourself why you do not delegate your responsibilities or get responsible for drawing your own boundaries. This can free you up for more success.

Page of Wands

A youth that has a message. New inspiration and new excitement about your life and energy for new endeavors.

King of Wands

The King of Wands may help you but, unlike the King of Cups, he will not go too far out of his way. He may be married so make sure you are careful about what you do with him. He can be a great business partner, but he will stay behind the scenes with others. He likes to shine for his own successes.

Queen of Wands

The queen is highly energetic, independent, and sexualized. She is a great partner if you can take her straightforward, no-nonsense ways.

Ace of Swords

The Ace of Swords is the sword of clarity. It can come with a sharp tongue or in a sudden and unexpected way. However, it only cuts through the illusion and trash you do not need clouding your vision.

Two of Swords

Indecision is what this card represents, and this is a refusal to see what the opportunities can bring. This person, just like the Eight of Swords to a lesser degree, has no idea they can just drop the swords and decide. They are afraid of choosing wrongly, unaware that they can go back if they feel they've made a mistake.

Three of Swords

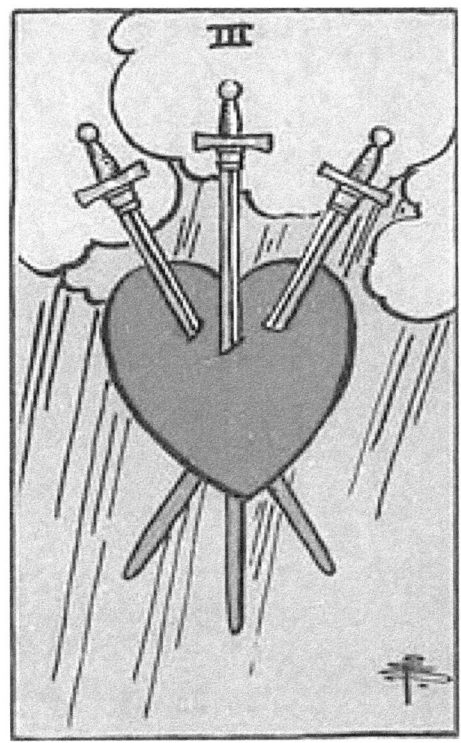

Like the three in any suit, this is the reaping of rewards. Your mental agility and perseverance have brought you to this great victory, but there is still much work to be done. Do not wait on it too long.

Four of Swords

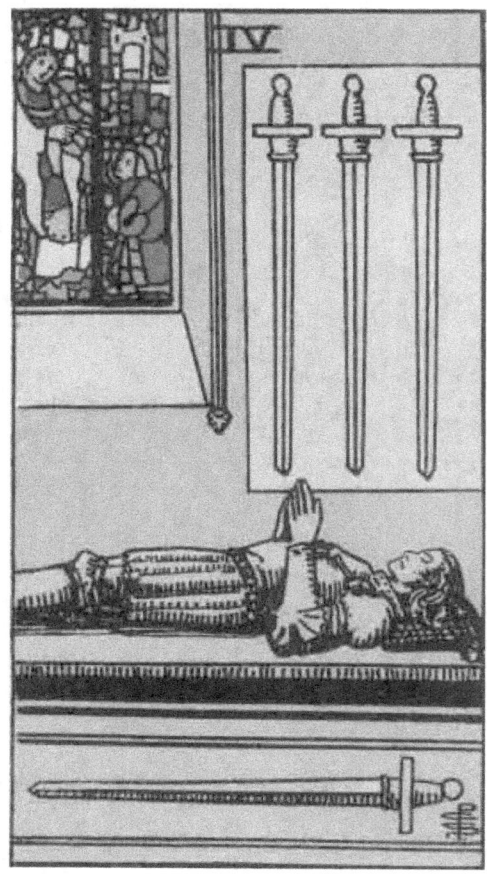

Rest and relaxation for the efforts of the first three swords is needed because you have exhausted not only your mental faculties, but your physical ones, too! Rest before you become ill. Your further achievements can wait.

Five of Swords

You have won the battle but maybe at the expense of the war? Have you had to resort to base tactics in order to get what you want from others? Today, you need to look at your inner world and see what you have created. What was the cause for this? Study the surrounding cards for the answer.

Six of Swords

Accepting help from others. You may be on your way to distant shores or anywhere other than where you are right now. This can be mentally or physically or both. Study the surrounding cards to be able to get a grip on the best itinerary or next steps if you are unsure where you are headed.

Seven of Swords

Is someone you know being sneaky, deceptive, or outright lying or stealing? Do you fall in that category? Karma is the work of the day here. Watch your back for theft in every form. Study the surrounding cards to find out what form it comes in.

Are you deceiving yourself? Why do you feel you need to keep your true self hidden? Are you in danger if you are authentic? If that is the case, then do another spread to find out what the issue is.

Eight of Swords

This is the card like the Two of Swords, but the indecision is based on 100% fear. The person is also blindfolded in most decks but there is a clear path to freedom. She cannot take it only because of her own blocks. Study the surrounding cards to find the block and bust it! Otherwise, the next two cards will turn you into a neurotic mess. It can be avoided.

Nine of Swords

The craziness of the last few sword card experiences has left you robbed of sleep and riddled with anxiety. Take an image of this spread you have done and then throw another spread with this card in the middle to find out the solution to the issue.

Ten of Swords

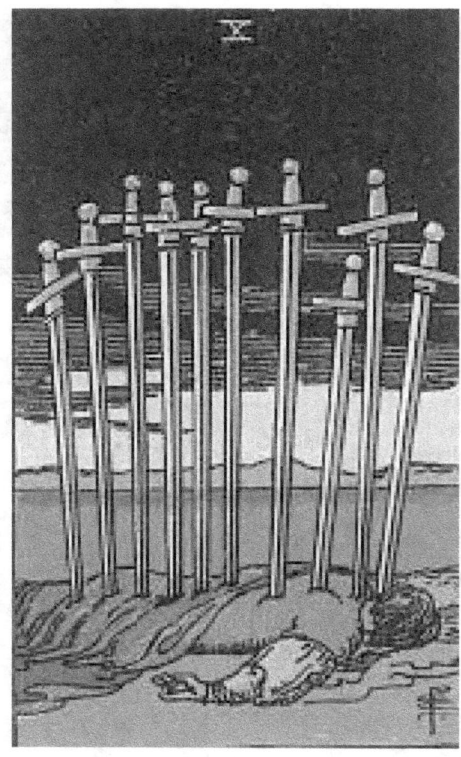

There is way too much on you now. Not heeding the warnings of the last few swords to sort out your fears and racing thoughts has now hit critical mass. You must do something to delegate responsibility, smash fear, and love yourself more than anyone or anything else. You are as low as you can go but look ahead to the rising sun that brings you new hope.

Page of Swords

A sharp-tongued youth or youthful person. Watch out for what they say, but don't take it too personally as this card is fraught with misunderstanding. It will get sorted out according to the surrounding cards.

King of Swords

The King of Swords is a controlling person but can be fair. He is analytical and can make a good partner so long as emotion is not something you are looking for.

Queen of Swords

She is cold and hardened by her life experience, yet she imparts so much wisdom. Listen to what she has to say and respect her. You will have a friend, confidant, and loyal companion for life. Do not let the cold exterior fool you. She is wise and discerning of all, and if you are upright and honest, she will be an asset to you. Infertility is a possibility with this card, but other cards must support it.

Ace of Pentacles

Your financial success prevails! You have either worked hard for it or it is falling from the clouds on to you, so be happy! Learn how to manage money so you can make it through or avoid the pitfalls of the following cards.

Two of Pentacles

Juggling and multitasking is the order of the day. Be aware though, that you may be juggling things that do not belong to you, or that you have taken on wanting to please yourself or others. Remember that the Pentacles are practical, and your plans need a practical plan between the Ace of Pentacles, when you receive your opportunities, and the Two of Pentacles.

Three of Pentacles

This is a card of collaboration and sharing the work with others. It is a time of enjoying your work as you create exciting things with each other! You may meet exciting and smart new people that can help give you opportunities.

Four of Pentacles

Do not hold onto the money you have made through the Three of Pentacles so tightly that you cannot invest further. Learn to create a plan and stick to it but also understand that business takes investment. Money in, money out.

Five of Pentacles

In case you have missed the lesson of the Four of Pentacles; you may be experiencing loss. This can be a loss in any area of life as with any of the cards but there is an overarching lesson here. You have help! Turn around and accept it now— it is waiting for you. Not everyone will hurt you. You are better than your fears so let go and use your intuition and discernment.

Six of Pentacles

There are those that wish to be charitable to you or those that you want to give charity to. The overall lesson of this card is to give generously and remember all that you must be grateful for. You would do well to investigate philanthropy.

Seven of Pentacles

You must remember that the seeds you plant are ripe to be sown when you patiently wait. A watched pot never boils, so while you wait you would do well to plan the next phase in your harvest.

Eight of Pentacles

You are the apprentice and learning a new craft or mastering your current one. Hard work pays off in the long run. Keep at it! New opportunities are simmering around the corner and people are watching you while you work. The right people!

Nine of Pentacles

You are the independent person who enjoys their garden and all that you have planted in it. You are OK with your lonesomeness. Mastering this card means that you know the difference between alone and lonely. You can also be a solo business owner, independently rich or a freelancer, or you will meet someone like this that will help you on your way.

Ten of Pentacles

You have the life you have always wanted and are enjoying your life with complete abandon. This is the end of a cycle and a new, fresh one begins! Marriage and/or children could be indicated if the surrounding cards support it.

Page of Pentacles

This is possibly a younger person that you are introduced to that will give you an opportunity. This could be business or mixing a bit of business with pleasure. They will be an important part of your journey. Be open to invitations. Use your intuition and discernment.

King of Pentacles

This is a hard-working masculine energy. So much so, that they may provide but not acknowledge your existence too much. This is a workaholic, but a great provider and business partner if nothing else.

Queen of Pentacles

This queen is a nurturer and is the Earthy, honest, and strong, quiet type. She knows how to stockpile her money and how to make it work for her while she shares her abundance with her household. She is an all-encompassing divine feminine.

PART 3: THE BEST TAROT SPREADS FOR BEGINNERS!

The Tarot spreads here have been hand selected from experience and are perfect for the beginner. Everything you will learn in this Tarot reading guide is designed to help you fully understand the best way to look at the Tarot. Instead of viewing it as a series of separate cards, you will see yourself, your life, and a complete journey in them.

The meanings were written that way here so you could get the wheels turning with the right Tarot reading habits. The spreads also follow a commonsense fluidity that you'll find quite easy to understand.

Let's get started!

Simple Spreads for Beginners!

These first spreads are simple and fun to get your feet wet with the cards and become more dialed into the cards with your intuition. There are three card spreads with the opportunity to pull clarification cards.

We suggest that no more than one at a time and a maximum of three clarifiers should be pulled per reading. Why? Because it will confuse a beginner too much.

The cards are meant to be broad, but not vague. To a beginner, it may seem so, but as you tune into the cards, you will start to see that they have specific messages. A good rule of thumb for clarification cards is that a cycle is the number nine.

So, if you choose more than nine clarification cards you start a new cycle or meaning in the case of the Tarot. We suggest no more than three so that you are not overwhelming yourself, nor are you changing the meaning of the cards.

Spread One | The Three Card: Past, Present, Future

This is a great spread to begin with. It tells a story from the querent's immediate past to the present and then the probable future. It is a great spread to begin with to see a story formulate. Then, we can move on to longer and longer spreads once you are used to it.

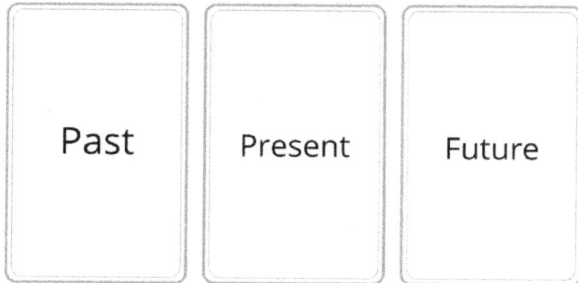

Instructions:

Go back to the first part of the guide where it tells you how to protect and create a sacred space. Have your deck cleaned and handy and make sure you will not be interrupted for an hour or so.

Once you are all set and ready, sit with your eyes closed and, with your question in mind, slowly shuffle the cards. **A note on shuffling:** You can look up easy ways to shuffle cards on YouTube.

No need to get fancy. All shuffling is for is to infuse your energy into them slowly and thoroughly and to change the order of the cards back to random after each reading. In your case, it is mixing them from being in the order they came in.

Don't worry if they are all still upright, you can't make a mistake. If one is meant to be overturned, then it will happen naturally by way of the Universe.

How to Formulate a Question:

Now, one note on the question. Don't make your questions too complex. The best way to ask a question is to phrase it like this:

"What will be so if I _____?" State your course of action in the blank space.

"What course of action should I take?"

"What is hidden from me?"

"What are my next steps?"

Keep it simple and state ONE question. Also, never state a question within a question or as an OR question. Here are some examples of bad question structures for the Tarot:

"When will I meet my husband, and will we be happy?"

"Should I move or stay here?"

We know you have probably been on YouTube and have seen all sorts of long questions and questions within questions. Most times this is for an algorithm and the reader's ratings. If you notice, they seem to all follow each other. In the real world this can get very confusing, and you could end up really frustrating yourself or the poor people you are reading for.

When you feel as if you should stop shuffling, open your eyes, and place the whole deck in front of you on the table. Sit a moment and recite the question again in your mind. With your left receptive hand cut the deck into three piles.

Sit again and breathe deeply. If you feel in a rush then stop yourself and take three deep, slow breaths with your eyes closed. Recite the question again and as you open your eyes you will be drawn to a pile.

This is your intuition and the key here is not to overthink the situation. Just pick that pile up and put the rest aside. Draw three cards from the top and place them left to right. Turn them over and interpret them. Reading the left for past, the middle for present, and the right for future.

Once you've read the meanings and assimilated what the "book meaning" is, we want you to look at the pictures. Don't think too hard. Write down what your gut is telling you.

Now, interpret what you think the answer is to your question. Keep a Tarot journal always. There is a template to use at the end of this section on spreads to help guide you with the most important sections of your Tarot journal.

When you do this spread, make sure you have a question that you do not have to wait long for the proof to manifest. Or ask it something you already know. Practice it a few times so you can prove to yourself that your answers are on target.

All About Love!

These are of course the most popular among teens. Every other week there is a new crush! Don't take it all too seriously. Test the waters of young life and practice with yourself and your friends.

Spread Two | The Relationship Spread

This one is great if you or someone you know is in a committed relationship for a while. It works well when the couple know each other well and they know what the other is apt to do. It's not good for dating or a new romance that's still in the discovery phase.

The Relationship Spread is also great for finding out if your interpretation of the answers is on target because you will be able to see it happen right before your eyes. You can also see things in your interactions with your partner.

Shuffle as per our instructions and do the right rituals.

Line the cards from left to right.

1. Left Card (Card 1): What binds you together.

This card represents what the force is that is keeping you together. It may be something positive or negative. Pull a clarification card up to no more than three times if the answer is unclear. DO NOT pull clarifiers just because you do not like or don't believe the answer, because it will come out wrong.

2. Middle Card: Solution.

This card is looked at last but kept in the middle as a focal point. Move on to card three first and observe the same exact instructions as for card one in this and all readings here.

Once you come to this card's meaning, it will tell you what the solution to your issues in card three are. Sometimes a separation is needed, like it or not, and sometimes you can work on it. Remember that this is Tarot for Teens, and if you are under age 18 it may be a bit much for you to take love so seriously right now. The Universe will ALWAYS guide you to what is in your highest good.

3. Right Card: What is against you.

This is what is going against you two or keeping you apart. Clarifiers are typically needed here but no more than three!

Spread Three | Love Triangle

This is great for when you already know your partner is with someone else and you're having a relationship on the side. At some point, in a healthy relationship the person who has the two people strung along needs to choose. Then, you need to see if their actions denote a one-time thing or a character flaw that you'll have to deal with when they have someone besides you—again.

7 Card Spread

```
  [1]   [2]   [3]
[4][5]    [6][7]
```

1. Card 1 (Left): Represents you.
2. Card 2: Represents the third party.
3. Card 3: How they decide between you.
4. Card 4 (Left): Their character.
5. Card 5: Is this a habit for them?
6. Card 6: Are they good for you?
7. Card 7: What you need to work on to stop attracting this kind of relationship.

Spread Four | Relationship Strengths and Weaknesses

8 Card Spread

```
  1     2     3

4  5  6  7  8
```

This is a great spread for working on an existing relationship. It takes a candid look at your influence over the relationship and your partner's, both positive and negative. Finally, you pull an advice card for both of you so you can work on raising the vibration of the relationship by working on yourself first.

1. Card 1 (Left): Your strengths as an individual.
2. Card 2: Your positive influence on the relationship.
3. Card 3: Your negative influence on the relationship.
4. Card 4 (Left): Their strengths as an individual.
5. Card 5: Their positive contributions to the relationship.
6. Card 6: Their negative influence on the relationship.
7. Card 7: End of row one. Your Overall Advice Card
8. Card 8: End of row two. Their Overall Advice Card

Practicing General Prediction Spreads

Spread Five | General Predictive Spread | Any Subject | Two Path Choice

Intermediate Level

This spread can be used for any issue. Its nature is predictive rather than therapeutic. It gives you two path choices and two distinctive outcomes. The cards are placed in two separate spreads side by side.

This spread will challenge you a bit more and take you to the intermediate level. This is where you can begin to use your intuition.

2 Pathway Spread

```
  1       4
  2       5
  3       6
```

1. Card 1, 2 and 3 represent pathway choice one in column one, left side of table: This is the story of the pathway for you to interpret.

    1. Card 4, 5 and 6 are opposite in column two and represent pathway choice two, right side of table: This is the story of the alternative pathway choice for you to interpret.
    2. After you've interpreted both pathways as far as you can, you can start pulling clarifying cards for this spread, up to six for each column.

Once you have a clear definition of both pathways, put the deck aside for a bit. Take your time and really look at the meanings of each card one column at a time. Start with column one and meditate on it. Relax and soften your vision. Now, look at them together left to right or top to bottom if you placed them that way. Then, do the next column the same way.

What is the story telling you? After you look at the 'book' meanings, write them down in a story-like summary. Now, look at them and write a summary of what you 'feel' it means.

Next, pull one card for each column. This is your advice. If there's something unclear, pull only one clarifier at a time and meditate on each. Choose no more than three for each pile.

So, why write it all down? You can put the journal aside and go back to it later to see which interpretation was correct!

We labeled the first few, apart from the Celtic Cross which can be used for any issue, as love spreads because they are looked at in a different way, but you can use any of the spreads for anything you want.

The number of cards and the extra position categories will allow you to gain a deeper look into any issue. We suggest using a love spread for love and looking at some of the court cards as characters in the beginning. This just makes things a bit easier for the learner.

Some of the spreads will have no specific category because intermediate to advanced readings will give you the chance to look at the suits and intuitively give them a meaning other than the obvious.

Let us explain:

Traditionally the Cups are emotions and associated with love; the Pentacles are money and material things, so they are associated with work or any way we earn; Wands are thoughts and Swords are action, or vice versa depending on the deck and your intuition.

Which brings us to our point. The next spreads you can intuitively work up to creating your own meanings according to your intuition.

For some of the spreads we will be using the same basic cross and each spread in the first section will add to that cross so you can get attuned to the shape and where all the 'core' cards go. Then, once you're confident enough, you can start to create your own spreads out of the basic cross.

This is Tarot for Teens so you can certainly start now to master the Tarot bit by bit and practice, practice, practice!

Important Instruction Before You Go Further

The Basic Cross

We will use the basic cross in order for you to easily construct each reading in this section, and then we'll tell you where to place extra cards. The meaning of the positions of the cross will stay the same for all the spreads in this section.

We will then add additional cards with different meanings. This is so you can choose what types of spreads would suit your issues once you get the hang of it. Use the cross below to start the rest of the spreads in this first section only.

The Basic Cross Layout:

Basic Cross Layout

1. Card 1 (Middle Position): The core issue and reason for asking the question.
2. Card 2 (Top of Card 1, crossing it): If you feel comfortable reading reversals: if the top of Card 2 is to the right it's to be read with the upright meaning. If it's to the left, it's to be read the opposite of the upright position meaning. For example, let's use the Magician. If you place the card across Card 1, and the Magician's head is pointing to the right, it's read in the upright position. If his head is pointed to the left, it's read as the reversed meaning.
3. Card 3 Immediate Past (Top of Cross): This represents something that is affecting the question.
4. Card 4 Immediate Future (Bottom of Cross): This represents something that is upcoming that will affect the result. For this position, if you don't like what this represents, look to the advice card to see how to change it.
5. Card 5 (Left of Cross): What action created your current circumstance. This card represents what action you took or that of the person you are reading for took to influence the situation.
6. Card 6 (Right of Cross): What is the likely outcome of the situation if you or they stay on the path they're on.

Consciousness and Spiritual Life and Gifts Spreads!

These spreads are fantastic for the beginner to tap into the spiritual gifts they have. They're fun and curious.

Spread Six | 10 Card Spread

Intermediate Spread

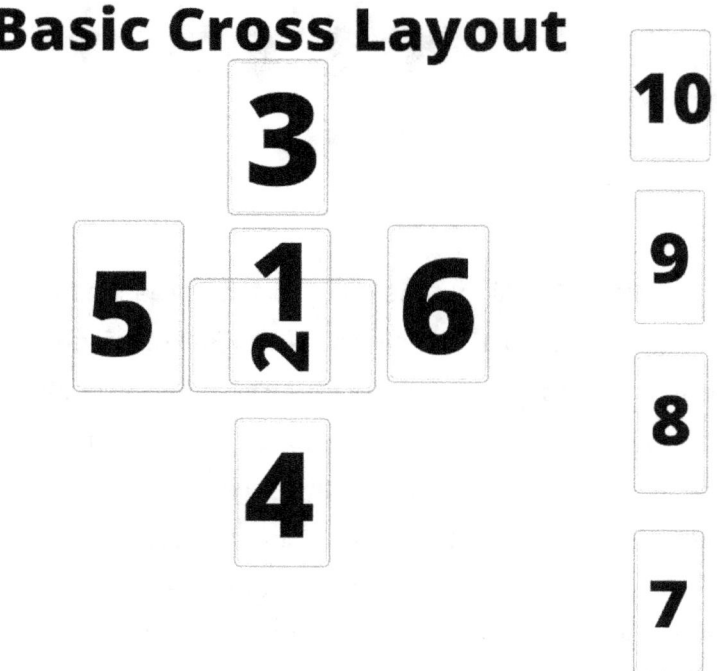

1. Card 1 through 6 creates the cross.
2. Once the cross is constructed for this reading, create a row beneath it left to right for the following card positions.
3. Card 6 (Right): What path may be better for you in this circumstance? This position will tell you what you should give up or take on to create a more effective pathway than the one you have now.
4. Card 7: What could potentially hinder that new pathway or what needs to be purged before you can take on that alternate pathway.
5. Card 8: The likely outcome if you take the new pathway.
6. This is what would likely happen if the new path were taken, and you purged what you were told to purge. This is one of the most important and telling cards. The result of your own free will actions can be your success!
7. Card 9: What is hidden about the subject. This position tells you what may be hidden in the situation. Don't ever fear this position because it will empower

you! No, you can't always control or stop certain events, but most things, if forewarned, you're forearmed.

8. Card 10 (Final): The final likely outcome if you choose to follow the advice given by all cards in the spread. Compare this card to Card 5 in the cross which tells you what the likely outcome is if you kept on the path you were on when you started the reading.

Spread Seven | State of Consciousness Spread

This spread is in the empowerment and predictive categories. It's good to note that all readings are both. You can predict, but without a problem and solution you can't grow. In this spread, you'll see what your own state of consciousness is and what type of environment you are creating for yourself.

It's best to look at yourself before looking at the outer reality because both you and your karmas are creating that. You can control a good part of it, but you must be aware first. So, let's go there now and try this one!

1. Card 1 through 5 creates the cross.
2. Once the cross is constructed for this reading, create a row beneath it left to right for the following card positions.
3. Card 6: What is the core issue with your state of consciousness that is affecting your situation? What is it consciously and subconsciously affecting your life and the smaller situation you're asking about? Once you can see this you have the power to make better choices.
4. Card 7: What things you don't see coming outside of you that may catch you off guard. This can be positive too by the way.
5. Card 8: What are you manifesting out of your state of consciousness? This position is a snapshot of what your state of consciousness is now manifesting in your reality.
6. Card 9: What you can do to improve your state of consciousness and your manifestation.
7. Card 10: The outcome should you follow the advice from Card 9.

Spread Eight | Your Spiritual Gifts Spread

This is a spread that gives you a snapshot into your own spiritual gifts. The basic cross is still used in this spread and this is how you use the information given in the basic cross first.

The position meanings don't change, but the way you use them does a bit. Here's the rule of thumb regarding the basic cross for the Your Spiritual Gifts Spread.

The basic cross will cover past, present, immediate future and possible outcome etc. Use each of these sections in a context of how your surroundings are right now. Then, we'll go into the extra cards that hone in on your special gifts!

It's a great thing to discover your spiritual gifts young while you're still a teenager! By the time you're a full-on adult you'll be able to use them to enhance your life, shape your future, and help others.

One thing we'll share with you is that you should never fear developing your gifts. When you have predictive gifts, which most of them can be used as such, people get uncomfortable with it because they feel they may see something that they don't like.

Just remember that training can tame the parts you don't like, so don't worry too much about that. Most people's spiritual gifts do not include that type of thing being an overarching feature. One word to the wise; don't watch too many psychic/horror movies to get your information.

Okay, let's get to this amazing 16 Card spread!

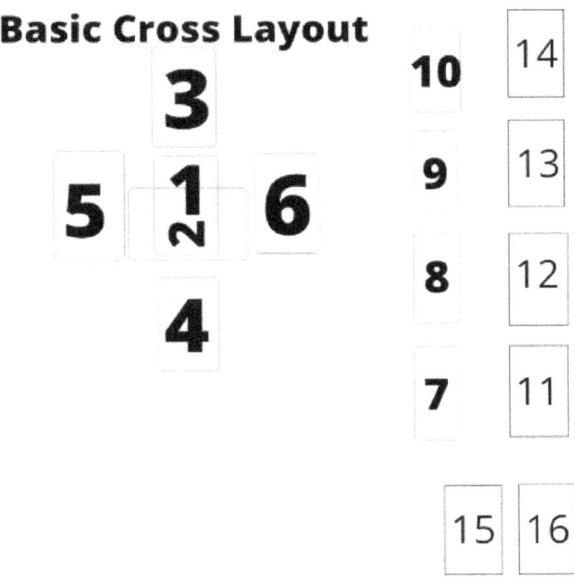

Card 1 through 6 creates the small cross.

Once the cross is constructed for this reading, create a row beside it with cards 7-10.

Cards 7 through 10 are: What types of spiritual gifts do you possess?

For the next 4 cards, 11 through 14, you'll separate the four suits, and put the rest aside. Separate the Cups, Swords, Wands, and Pentacles.

You don't have to put them in order, just separate them and shuffle each pile for each suit and pull one card from each. What order you shuffle and pull them is up to you—no rules. For instance, Cups then Wands then Pentacles then Swords or a completely different random order. This is a way for you to develop your intuition.

Now, create another row for the next four cards 11-14 directly **beside** the column of cards beside the cross numbered 7-10. This column is numbered 10, 11, 12, 13. So, card 10 is next to card 7; card 11 is next to card 8; card 12 is next to card 9 and card 13 is next to card 10. SEE DIAGRAM. The order is important as you are further describing each of your gifts in Cards 7, 8, 9 and 10. The cards can now be placed back in the deck. We suggest giving them a good shuffle before you begin again.

After you interpret those, take your time as always, then you'll choose the last two cards, Cards 15 and 16. Card 15 is what is blocking your gifts and Card 16 is what you can do about it. For these, you can actually do two to three clarification cards each, but we don't suggest more than that because then it confuses the answers.

These next spreads will be six card spreads. The shape is that of a triangle.

The three cards that make up the base of the triangle will be Cards 1, 2, and 3 and the three cards that make up the point of the triangle are Cards 4, 5, and 6.

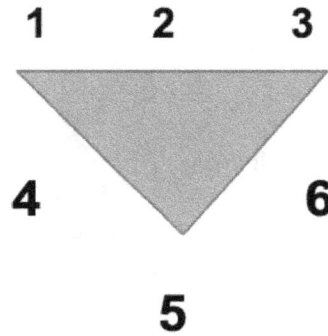

Home, Practicality Spread

We included this bonus spread because it's popular and a little more advanced so it's a great tool to develop intuitive reading skills.

Spread Nine | Best Type of Place to Live for Me!

We thought this would be a useful one for you to use because so many people are looking to move out of their area or even their country to find the right space for them.

Use the above triangle to cast your spread:

- Card 1: Your mindset now and how it affects your view of where you live now. Sometimes we may be bored or in an emotional state or maybe we associate where we live with some trauma. Find out what's really making you want to flee your home so you can make the best choice.

- Card 2: The state of your surroundings. This covers the people and general atmosphere of your surroundings.
- Card 3: Where your ideal living situation would be. You already know this on some level.
- Card 4: How to get where you need to be and what blocks you.
- Card 5: What is in your favor with your moving plans.
- Card 6: Overall advice.
- Clarification cards when needed.

All About Timing! When and How Things may Happen Spreads

These spreads are a great tool for learning how to time things for beginners. They're simple and easy to understand. As you become more in tune with the cards, you'll be able to intuit the timing more. You will use the seasons here to make things easier.

Typically, the Minor Arcana is used to tell timing, but here you will use the seasons in the court cards so be prepared to remove the court cards a few times and then return them to the deck for the rest of the reading. If you have more than one deck you can be clever about it and just take the court cards from that one to make things easier.

Use the triangle to cast your spread.

Spread Ten | Best Time to Make a Big Change?

- Card 1: Your current situation.
- Card 2: How your surroundings affect you.
- Card 3: How ready you are for a big change.
- Card 4: What's blocking you.
- Card 5: What's going for you.

- Card 6: General advice.

Spread Eleven | Next 7 Days?

- Card 1: Your general situation today.
- Card 2: What you aren't aware of coming your way.
- Card 3: What you have to be prepared for.
- Card 4: Opportunities being offered.
- Card 5: What and who to beware of and why.
- Card 6: Overall advice.

Spread Twelve | Next 30 Days?

- Card 1: The tone of today through the next seven days.
- Card 2: What you need to head off, so the week goes more in your favor.
- Card 3: What and who to beware of.
- Card 4: Action you must take now to create a positive month.
- Card 5: Should you make any big decisions this month?
- Card 6: Overall advice.

Spread Thirteen | Next 3 Months?

- Card 1: The tone of today and the next 30 days.
- Card 2: What to head off before the first month ends.
- Card 3: What action you must take in the next 60 days.
- Card 4: What you need to postpone and in what area of life you need to postpone for the next 90 days.
- Card 5: What goals will you reach by the next 90 days?
- Card 6: Overall advice.

Spread Fourteen | Six Months?

- Card 1: What you need to change in the next 60 days to get the remaining four months to go in your favor.

- Card 2: What you need to act on now.
- Card 3: What you need to act on or focus on for the next three months.
- Card 4: What you need to postpone, reflect on, or reevaluate for the next three months. You may use up to nine clarification cards for this. When you are clear and satisfied then move to the next two cards.
- Card 5: What you must act on for the remaining three months.
- Card 6: Overall advice.

Spread Fifteen | Year Ahead?

- Card 1: Overarching theme for the new year.
- Card 2: What you may consider giving up this year.
- Card 3: Overarching focus for the first six months.
- Card 4: Overarching focus for the remaining six months.
- Card 5: Results if you continue on the path you're on.
- Card 6: Overall advice to improve from the path you're on to something better.

People of Note! All About People in Your Life, Both Known and Unknown and Their Influence on Your Life Spreads.

These spreads are meant to shine light on the people around you and the environment you are in every day. They cover people you love, like, dislike, and may be meeting soon.

Use this spread to monitor the people around you and to become aware of how others may view you and how they may feel about you. Are they there to give you opportunities? Do you have soul or karmic contracts with them? What do they bring to the table and can you deal with them or should you?

These spreads will teach you how to recognize people in the cards as characters. They'll show you how to use the court cards separately and get used to their vibe.

Spread Sixteen | Who is my Next Love Partner?

For this spread, separate the court cards from the deck. Shuffle all the court cards from all four suits together in one stack. Then choose Card 1 and Card 2. Then return them to the deck.

Shuffle the deck again and choose the rest of the cards. Keep the question in mind while you do this again. You may shuffle once for Card 1 and then again for Card 2. When you are done choosing cards 1 and 2 place them back in the deck. Once they are back in the deck; shuffle once to remix the court cards into the deck well enough so they come out randomly and not still in order. Then, concentrate on the question and choose the rest of the Cards 3 through 6 from the top of the deck.

- Card 1: Do you know this person already?
- Card 2: What are their strongest features? NOTE: Gender does not have to matter here. Whenever we use court cards for people, it's their energy and not their gender. A male can come out as a queen just as easily as a female and vice versa.
- Card 3: What occupation may they have?
- Card 4: Where might I meet them?
- Card 5: When will I meet them? This can be told by taking out the court cards again or by using the Minor Arcana. The Minor Arcana will give you days, weeks, or months. The court cards will give a season. You can use both and leave the Major Arcana aside. This will give you an opportunity to use your intuition because there is much argument as to what suit will give the day, month, or years. Some argue that Pentacles, since they are slow, Earthy, and deliberate are years.

However, we've seen this differently many times. We suggest for beginners to use the court cards and get the season—which on the Rider-Waite deck is marked clearly on the card. A good rule of thumb for beginners is to match them like this and set the intention while shuffling for the cards to answer you this way.

- Cups – Summer
- Wands – Spring

- Swords – Fall
- Pentacles – Winter
- Card 6: How to approach this person. Here you can get a feel for who they are and their character. Feel your way through this card so you can tell if they'll be good for you, and pull three clarification cards but no more so you don't confuse yourself.

Spread Seventeen | Are they Friend or Foe?

For this spread, you are trying to find out if someone is a friend or a frenemy or purely not for you. If you want to find out who your friends and enemies are, you can use this spread too. For that, you can take out the court cards and use them as you did in the love spread to find out who your next person is going to be. We suggest that you choose up to three cards for three people and then pull the six cards for each person. If you already know who it is and you are asking about this one person, then choose one court card only first before choosing the next six below.

- Card 1: How does this person feel about you?
- Card 2: Why do they feel the way they do?
- Card 3: What event either brought them to love or dislike you?
- Card 4: What you can do to get closer to them or cut the cord to them.
- Card 5: Is this a karmic contract you must finish or is it finished?
- Card 6: Overall advice.

Now, remember we said that you never ask a question in a question when addressing the Tarot. Just so you understand that we aren't contradicting ourselves here. With the overall question you don't do that but with the meanings of each position you can. Why is this so? Because you'll know by the card that shows up if they are friend or enemy in this case, or what brought them to love or dislike you.

Spread Eighteen | Next BFF?

For this one you can also use the court cards to find out who your next BFF is going to be. Maybe they're already associated with you or they're showing up soon!

- Card 1: What are their strongest features?
- Card 2: Do I already know them?
- Card 3: How will I know them?
- Card 4: Where will I meet them?
- Card 5: What is your soul or karmic contract with them?
- Card 6: How should you approach this relationship? This is where you can feel out if this person offering this relationship with you is good for you. Remember though that if the cards indicate a karmic contract you may not want to walk away. Pull some cards to clarify what type of effect this person will have on you and what you'll gain from it.

Spread Nineteen | People at My Next Job?

Again, pull the court cards just to see the overall look so you can recognize them. Since they're strangers and you haven't and probably won't invest in them much yet, if at all, you'll want to just do a simple spread. Just take note of the court cards and the features and character of each.

- Card 1: How will I be received?
- Card 2: Why will I be received this way?
- Card 3: How can I make my work surroundings comfortable?
- Card 4: Will I meet someone special at work?
- Card 5: How should I best approach my workmates?
- Card 6: Overall advice.

All About the Bag! Your Career, Money, and Material Pathway Spreads

These spreads take care of your material life. Your business, business partnerships, the people at work, and decisions regarding career pathway.

Spread Twenty | Next Business Partner?

Choose a court card for this person.

- Card 1: What is their strongest feature?
- Card 2: Where will you find your next business partner?
- Card 3: What is the karmic or soul contract you have with them?
- Card 4: What role are they meant to play in your partnership?
- Card 5: Result of your business with this person?
- Card 6: Overall advice.

Spread Twenty-One | Stay or Go Career?

- Card 1: Why your current situation is not working.
- Card 2: Why you should change your career path or something about your current one.
- Card 3: Do you need to leave your current situation at all?
- Card 4: Results from changing your current situation.
- Card 5: Results if you don't change your current situation and just improve it.
- Card 6: Overall best advice. Use your intuition and the rest of the cards to figure out if you'll do well to stay or go.

Spread Twenty-Two | How Will I Make My Money?

- Card 1: What's the best field or outlet for me to make money in?
- Card 2: What's the first step to the field or outlet?
- Card 3: What is blocking me from that pathway?
- Card 4: What can I do about any blocks to that pathway?
- Card 5: Results if I follow this new pathway indicated by the cards and clear any blocks.
- Card 6: Overall advice.

Spread Twenty-Three | Should I Work for Myself?

- Card 1: Should I work for myself?
- Card 2: What type of business should I have?
- Card 3: Should I fly solo or get a business partner?
- Card 4: How will working for myself enhance my life?
- Card 5: How will working for myself change my life?
- Card 6: Overall advice.

Spread Twenty-Four | Is There a Future in My Career?

- Card 1: What about my career is not working?
- Card 2: What about my career is working?
- Card 3: Why am I working where I am now?
- Card 4: Is there a future here that would make me happy?
- Card 5: Is there an alternative to working that would make me happier?
- Card 6: Overall advice.

Spread Twenty-Five | Am I on the Right Path?

Just a note about how to use this spread. There's no such thing as a path that is right or wrong. There's only where you are and that's where you're supposed to be; however, if you're enlightened about the path you're on, you can choose to make it one that makes you happy or choose to change it. That is how you use this spread.

- Card 1: What is it on my current path that isn't working?
- Card 2: What is it on my current path that is working?
- Card 3: Should I change my current path or just make improvements to it? Clarification cards will be needed for this for beginners.
- Card 4: What's my best step forward?
- Card 5: Should I seek a mentor for more information?
- Card 6: Overall advice.

PART 4: TAROT MAGIC! MANIFESTATION AND GROWTH RITUALS WITH THE TAROT

This next section is a fun and informative section on Tarot and what you can do with it apart from prediction. You'll learn how to manifest and how to grow spiritually using the Tarot. You were exposed to spiritual gifts and spiritual growth reading just to give you a taste of how the Tarot can help you grow.

The Tarot as the Story of Life

The Tarot as we mentioned before, is a story of life from birth to death with all the cycles and everyday lessons in between. This makes it easy to read the cards when we use them to predict, but you can use them as representations in the Universe to manifest and to actually make things happen by manipulating energy with them.

The Universe runs on symbols and emotion and not on words. We'll get into that when we get to spell work. The Tarot has thousands of years of energy from everyone that has used them and everyone that is still using them all over the world. That energy is what makes each card a kind of thought form with an energetic life of its own.

When you evoke these energies, you'll see things take place in your life according to the story you tell in the way you place the cards on your table in your sacred space.

Before we get started, there are a few important things to note before you perform any undertaking. This first section covers myths about magic. We covered myths about Tarot, but magic and ritual have more misunderstanding than anything else.

Since this is a guide for teens, we feel it especially important that you get your information from credible and logical sources rather than some random YouTube channel or elsewhere.

The first thing to remember is that magic and ritual have always been tied to some kind of ridiculous darkness when it's not all that different than prayer. A manipulation of energy only means that you are tapping into the Divine source and there's nothing dark about that.

Magic, ritual, and divination were used in societies as a normal way of living, but it empowered people. When society became more politically oriented and money and power came into play, well, then magic and ritual were demonized to control the masses.

Today, we have a more open world situation where we don't have to fear having a different belief system. We also have a greater understanding of metaphysics and the spiritual nature of man. We have no law that states we have to be any one religion, etc. In some countries, it's still this way but very few and we hope this continues to change as people awaken.

Myths About Magic

Rituals and Magic are only for high priests and priestesses or some high-ranking, trained magician.

This is not true. Magic is there for all of us because it's from nature, and because it's natural, the wisdom belongs to all of us. You're young, and when you begin to be open to the mysteries of life, you'll attract all sorts of people if you join groups or communities.

Always beware of people that will tell you that they have knowledge only for them. Also beware of those who want to put you in a hierarchy. You can practice magic and ritual by yourself or with friends you trust without a cult-like situation where you could be open to abuses. This should be an exciting and curious time for you.

Rituals and Magic have to be done in a very precise way in order to work and you need to make sure you don't mess up.

This is also wrong. There really isn't, in our opinion, any way to mess it all up. Not with sympathetic, practical magic.

That is the type of magic and ritual you do with Tarot as a beginner and a teenager. You'll never be called into high-magic or anything deeper because that would be overload right now. In that case it is precise but comes with its own set of problems you don't need.

Ritual and Magic can't be done without years of intensive training.

That goes along the same lines of the other myths. There is no school of magic you need to go through.

Ritual and Magic changes your life because it opens portals and now you can't turn back from the spirits that know who you are.

This kind of thing is really from myths propagated by two things: Hollywood movies and very extreme religions. Neither are healthy and you needn't have the fear. If you decide you never want to touch a card or a ritual ever again, you most certainly can walk away from it all.

The other reason why some think that you can't walk away, or your life will change is because once you gain the wisdom of the Universe, it's kind of hard to go back to 'sleep' as we say; and it's okay if you don't want to, it's healthy. It means your eyes are wide open and you are ready to learn and grow!

Rituals and Magic need tools that are expensive and you have to learn to use them all precisely.

You can use tools, or you can use your mind. You don't even need the cards. The tools are there to call up emotions and those emotions and symbols are sent out to the Universe to do what you need them to do. It's as simple as that.

Magic is done all the time, every day by everyday people. You have done it yourself and it's funny to think of, but people who are dead set against magic, ritual, and Tarot do it all the time. Every time you pray, or talk to God, or even think heavily about anything and attach emotion to it—you are doing magic!

You can curse, hex, or otherwise harm another through magic or ritual.

Well, we aren't in the school of thought that this is possible as we all have a Divine protection. The person would have to know about it, and they would have to believe. It goes against every natural law to be able to physically influence a person to that extent.

Furthermore, where one looks for trouble, one will find it. The law of attraction will turn whatever negative or positive you cast out to someone back to you three times or more. Karma doesn't play. It has no conscience; it just serves justice. So, in this guide we don't even entertain such a thing and we suggest you not taint your blossoming young life with anything but positive work.

Okay, so we think this should be straight on the truth about magic and we can now get started with the work section.

Beginner Tarot Magic for Manifesting Everyday Things

In this section, we will teach you several magic rituals for growth and manifestation. We won't have to separate them into topics. For example: we won't do Tarot magic to manifest a job and get specific. There are too many cards in the deck and so many combinations that we don't want to overwhelm you.

The easiest way to learn will allow you the freedom to create on your own and use this guide as just that—a guide as learning principles and mechanics.

Let's get started!

How to Cast Your Tarot Rituals Effectively.

Important: Do Not Skip!

When using the moon phases that are made to bring something to you, you'll use the Waxing and Full. These are two of the basic phases; yes, there are more, but we don't need them here or for beginners, and we'll need the wording to be precise.

Now, before we told you that ritual doesn't need to be precise in the myths section. And the ritual you use doesn't; however, the wording you use will need to evoke the correct emotions the Universe will understand.

When the Universe *feels* your emotion, it will give you exactly what you are feeling as a result. So, if you *want* something, that word comes with an emotion. That emotion says, "I don't have this thing I am asking for"; therefore, it will keep it from you. It's an emotion of lack.

We learn from praying in the religious sort of way that we are asking for permission for something. When you manifest, it's different. Not that prayer doesn't work sometimes, but it takes a lot longer.

The feeling you want is that of already having it. What would it feel like if you already had what you have been seeking? Find a way to really get to that feeling before you have the object of your desire and see what happens! Then remember to let it go to the Universe. Don't stuff up the energy by working too hard. It has been said by some experts that 17 seconds of that feeling is all you need to make it all happen.

If you find yourself slipping into the less positive direction or doubting, then go 'neutral,' meaning don't fight it. Just let the thoughts flow out and don't get upset, it's normal! Going neutral means that you think of something totally unrelated to your spell. Have a cat or a dog? Pet it. Think of something joyful or neutral in emotion while you are manifesting.

New and Waning Moon Phases

The new moon is when the moon falls dark in preparation for it to begin its new light. In this phase you are setting the intention for what you want. At this time, you can forget emotion. Just go with it. It's okay to want. You are only intending what you want.

This is the time to journal it and also purge any emotions you think may get in the way. Teenagers are prone to moods and that's completely normal. Use this time all the way up until the moon begins to Wax. Talk about any of the doubts and fears and then intend better for yourself. This is also a self-care time. Take ritual baths, rest, and meditate.

The Waning moon is the phase that begins just after full. It's the time to banish things from your life that no longer serve you. The wording and emotion you use here is particularly important. If you push anything away or state what you *don't want* the Universe will give that which you do not want. Same principle as before, but even more important. Just feel what it feels like to be free of it. Feel the relief and gratitude.

Divine Timing

Each of us has a lifepath, positive and negative karmas and contracts to work out with people and situations. This is part of the reason why some manifestations happen quickly, and others seem to take their time; and yes, sometimes they won't work at all. You have a spiritual team that watches what

happens and though you have free will, it seems the Divine creator, or whatever force is comfortable for you to acknowledge exists, will have the last say on it.

Just remember that nothing will ever be stopped that was not for your highest good!

The Moon Phase Guide

When using the moon phases, it's best to keep a journal to write your intentions for anything you want or need, or want to banish or be rid of in your life. If you have a grimoire, then it too can be used. A grimoire is a book of personal spells, rituals, your readings, and magic recipes. It's a perfect thing to use for your Tarot rituals.

Waxing Moon: This is when the moon is growing toward full. The best way to use this moon phase is to begin to manifest the new intentions you created in the new moon. In your journal or grimoire, state what you are wanting as if it's already done. If you skipped or don't remember, it's important to read the previous section.

Full Moon: This is when the moon is obviously full, and you won't see any darkness in it. There is a shadow phase of a few days before and after going from one moon phase to the next where you may still use the energy. The full moon is for the realization or manifestation of the things you asked for in the waxing moon that you intended during the new moon. You can really cause an uptick in manifestation during this phase!

Waning Moon: This phase happens shortly after the moon is full. As soon as the next day you can begin breaking down anything you don't want. There are some good rules of thumb though for dealing with anything you don't want in the section before this.

New Moon: This phase is used to create the intentions for the rest of the month, months, or years depending on how big the request is. There's never any request too large for the Universe, but it does work on its own time.

Tarot Magic Ritual One: Manifesting in the Physical

This principle is for manifesting in the physical rather than working on yourself—that's next. Money, love, career, and anything you can physically acquire can be done with Tarot.

What You'll Need:

For this first Tarot magic ritual, you'll need only your Tarot cards and a small white candle, incense, sea salt, and water if you wish.

Steps:

1. Create the sacred space where you'll be able to leave the cards and any tools you may use such as candles and incense. Make sure the cards won't be disturbed for as long as you need them there. The space should be at least semi-private and not somewhere that prying eyes can see what you're doing, like kids and roommates. You can cover the cards with an altar cloth or natural covering of some sort if need be.
2. Reserve a private time when you won't have interruptions. You need to be able to sit and shuffle the cards and infuse your intention, then meditate and do the whole thing without disturbing your good vibration.
3. Sit at your table in your sacred space and close your eyes. Breathe deeply and let go of the day and any thoughts that are exhausting or negative. Evoke protection from the Universe only for now. As we said at the beginning of the book in the preparation section, don't evoke beings for now.
4. Shuffle the cards with your intention first to gain wisdom about your intention to manifest. Ask the cards for advice and insight about the work you are about to do. When you're satisfied and have made any changes the cards may have advised, then you may proceed.

Just a side note: The cards may, at times, tell you it's best to wait for now. It happens. The Universe never lies or misleads. Take whatever good advice they give you on timing.

5. Choose a significator card that represents you and place it in the middle. If you are doing the work for another then use a card that represents them. You can do this by the look of them or the personality or zodiac sign and match it to a court card.
6. Take the deck and choose the card suits and Major Arcana that represent what you have in mind.

For example: If you are wanting to manifest a job or money or something tangible like a car, use Pentacles; for emotions, love, and friendship, use Cups; for communication and swift action or movement, like moving houses, use Wands; and for legal issues, use Swords. Those are just examples; we encourage you to learn the meanings.

7. Place the card that represents what you want in the middle directly over the card that represents you. Not crossways horizontally like in the readings, but vertically to cover you.
8. Now, stop a few moments and stare at the picture in the card. Something magical starts to happen. Soften your eyes and don't blink a lot. Just relax your vision.
9. You'll see the pictures on the card start to change and morph into different shapes and even start to disappear in sections. Relax your body and posture and feel in your emotions a belief that this object you want is physically merging with you! The magic is already starting to happen!
10. Next, choose a card that matches the outcome you want. How exactly do you want the result to be? What do you want out of it? For example, you want a new job so you can get a house. Choose a card like the Ten of Pentacles or Ten of Cups if you want a family or marriage aspect. You can also use the Four of Wands as well. You can choose as many cards as you deem appropriate.
11. Now, breathe deep and let go. Do the same exercise as you did with the previous cards. Merge them all in your vision and your emotions. This time make certain you really feel it. Feel like you would if you really had what you wanted. Now, let it go and do the work. You can leave it put together from waxing to full moon for best results.

Important Note: Make sure when you feel like you already have the manifestation you don't ask, plead, or beseech anything or anyone for it. Also, don't feel the emotion of WANT.

The Universe will only give you what you feel; if you feel want, more *want* is what it will give you—you'll never acquire what you want. Understand? Only have the emotion of already having attained it and you win!

Tarot Magic Ritual Two: Manifesting for Physical Things

For those that are into the tools that create a great ambiance and vibration and that have the private space to do it, this ritual includes candles and the moon. You'll need to know at least the four main phases which are: waxing, full, waning, and new. These phases are responsible for our moods and the way our minds work here on Earth. They're also responsible for the manipulation of the Universe to do our bidding.

What You'll Need:

For this Tarot magic ritual, you'll need your cards, a white candle, incense of your choice and of course, your cloth to cover your cards for privacy if needed.

Steps:

1. Look at the meaning of the cards in the Major Arcana.
2. Write down the cards you'll use that match your manifestation.
3. Don't pull the cards yet.
4. Perform the cleansing and meditation rituals as prescribed here.
5. Shuffle the cards to get in tune with them. Take as long as you need.
6. Ask for a card that will tell you anything you need to know about what you're asking for. Pull from the top of the deck when you feel you should stop shuffling.
7. Use your intuition in order to see if it feels right, or you need to make any changes.

8. Pull the card you've chosen to represent you, called the significator. It can be any card, but since you'll want to use the card meanings freely, just choose one of the court cards to represent you or the person you may be doing the work for.
9. Pull the magician card and the moon card and place them both directly over your significator card vertically.
10. Sit and think of what you want just as you did in ritual one. Soften your vision and allow the cards to merge in your slightly blurred vision.
11. Take three deep cleansing breaths and light the white candle with your intention in mind and feeling as if you have it already.
12. Take the cards you chose to represent what you want and place them in a circle around the center cards.
13. Repeat: "And So It Is" three times with a breath in-between.
14. To close the spell, you may extinguish the candle, snuff it out, but never blow as it may be disrespectful to the fire elemental assisting you. Cover the cards with the cloth and clap, snap your fingers, or ring a bell three times.
15. You are now done. Think no more of it until the next moon phase comes. Then collect your cards, place them back in the deck, clean them, and do the next spell when you need to.

You can use those two Tarot magic rituals for anything you want at all. One is a bit shorter, and one is more involved and takes a bit more energy to perform. You can create your own from here. In the specific spell workbook in the next section, we've made a template for your practice, and we encourage more creativity, and less dogma and hard and fast rules.

The whole point of using the Tarot is to tell a story to the Universe about what you want to bring in and what you want to do without in your life and back it up with your emotions. That's as simple as what it is. The sky's the limit with what you can do if you keep in mind how to feel and how to set your mind; you can't mess up how to use the cards.

Other Ways to Use the Cards for Manifestation

For Attracting Money:

Carry a Pentacle card that represents money to you in your wallet. If you're really into the Tarot magic rituals, we encourage you to have a few decks. You can get mini decks online so you can carry them in your wallet and wear on you as a Talisman. A Talisman is a magically charged object or jewelry that is worn on the body or someplace close to the person for a specific purpose.

For Successful Apprenticeship:

Draw the Eight of Pentacles and the Ten of Pentacles and place them in your school case or business briefcase or where you work or study at home. Use the Tarot Magic Ritual One instructions.

For Attracting Love:

If you know the person you want to attract, then you would pull your significator and one for them. Do all the steps in the Tarot Magic Ritual One, then meditate each night with the cards on your altar from waxing moon to full moon. Light a pink candle, or white if you don't have access to pink or you've run out, for when you meditate.

Remember the law of attraction and feelings while you meditate. You already have them. By the full moon, place the cards under your mattress with the Ace of Cups until the next waxing moon. If they are for you and for your highest good, they will come to you. If not, something better will arrive.

The reason why we don't use the Lovers in this case is that it's more about choice and other things may cause confusion. The Ace of Cups is the beginning of a relationship in this case that is well balanced. You want that instead of something uncertain.

For Changing Jobs:

Find the right career when you already have one you don't like. Perform the cleansing and meditation practice, as well as the steps in Tarot Magic Ritual One, and do this with a card that represents the career you now have. Pull the Death card and place it over that card. Merge them in the usual meditation. Do this during the waning moon to the new moon. Keep the cards on your altar for the duration.

Don't meditate on the cards, just let the Universe do the work for this half of the spell and don't even think much about it. If you find yourself doing so, feel a joyful sense of expectancy that you'll have a new job soon! And not because you HATE this one. Bypass that feeling.

On the new moon, sit with your journal and describe the job you want. Tear the page out and place it face down under a white candle. Light it and meditate on that nightly for a few minutes each night until the waxing moon.

On the waxing moon, choose the Tarot card or cards that represent the job you want. Then, pull the Ace of Pentacles, Eight of Wands, and the Ace of Cups and replace the Death card pile you chose.

Place the old ones back in the deck and shuffle them until you feel the energy has dissipated. Keep the new cards on the altar until the full moon. Repeat the process each month until you get the job. Remember though, you need to be applying and get yourself out there so the Universe can guide the right people to you!

To Make a Work, School, or Home Atmosphere Friendlier:

Having issues with bullies, bad teachers, or parental issues? Perform the preparation as usual before each spell. Pull your significator card. Pull the cards that represent harmony. Choose the ones that resonate with you. Our suggestions if you're stuck are the Two of Cups with the Ace of Cups and the Three of Cups.

This takes care of love, celebration, partnership, and camaraderie. You can use the Ten of Cups if your family at home is the focal point, along with the Ten of Pentacles.

Do this spell when the moon is at the end of the new phase on the first day of waxing. Do it as you would following Tarot Magic Ritual One.

To Make Yourself More Attractive to Others:

If you want others to notice you in a more positive way, you can use the cards to actually build yourself up from the inside. This means you'll have to be open to change. Since you're a teenager, you're still growing and developing.

This is a great spell to cast upon yourself. The characters of the Queen of Cups and the Queen of Pentacles are two great character avatars to merge together to do the preparation as prescribed here and in the Tarot Magic Ritual One instructions.

Make the feeling that of acceptance of all the good qualities of the two queens. If you do have a smaller deck, carry the two cards with you and connect with them daily. Do this spell on the waxing to full moon and repeat, as necessary.

You can start creating your own now. The main principle is to be able to identify the cards and what their traditional meaning is as well as begin to intuitively study them. Then, once you feel your way to a card and match it to what you want to bring in or remove from your life, you can do the spell in any way you want.

The benefit of the magic practice with cards is that you'll become the best reader ever! The best readers can look at a card and know the meaning that it represents to them regardless of the book's meaning and still be accurate. In fact, many intuitive readers are even more accurate than those that go by the book alone.

We don't suggest starting out as a beginner without also knowing the basic book interpretations because it's a great way to get them in tune with you. You'll also know how the cards represent the cycle of life as we discussed in What Tarot Really Is.

In the next section we'll give you simple guidance as to what intuition is, how to recognize it, and how to use it with the cards. The rest is practice. We just want you to understand as much as you can about intuitive reading.

PART 5: INTUITIVE TAROT READING

So, how would we describe intuition? Intuition is sort of a feeling that happens in the body more than the mind. Not a physical sensation as such, although for some it is. That's why we can't tell you exactly what intuition feels like. It's one of those mysteries of being a spiritual being in a human body. What we can do is guide you through a few exercises. Since you're young, this is a great time to learn this—you aren't full of bias and too much skepticism from life yet.

Let's get started!

Discovering Your Intuition

Before we get into the card reading, we'll need you to exercise your intuition. One of the things we urge you to do is to get on YouTube and search Pick A Card Tarot Readings. In case you didn't already know, there are literally thousands of readers on YouTube with channels that do collective, group Tarot readings. You must choose a pile and in that pile is your reading.

There are thousands of people watching so your one pile is also for many others. The law of attraction, synchronicity, and destiny is at work here. It will be accurate because only the people that have the circumstances covered in that deck will be drawn to it—intuitively! If one pile does not resonate with you, then go back and choose another one. This is great practice and you'll be flexing your intuitive muscle in no time.

You can also do this for yourself and practice with your own deck. Think of something you want to know that is not too complicated. Set the intention while shuffling that one of the three or more cards you will place face down will have your answer. You won't see the cards until you turn them over.

While they lay face down, pass your eyes or hands or whatever you feel you should over the deck. Your intuition is when you just feel like that's the one! Turn it over and read the card. If it makes sense then you've got it, and if it didn't then you need more practice.

In fact, you'll never really stop practicing. It's good to challenge yourself regularly. There's a process we suggest. When you miss the mark and the card or reading you choose is not the right one, instead of jumping to the next reading, stop and think about it.

What was the feeling or sensation that made you choose the card you did? Try to pin it down. Was it your mind? Did you overthink it? Were you attracted to another card and then didn't go with your first instinct?

Some YouTube readers will use crystals or other fun objects on the cards. Some will use numbers and others will use a sound for each one. In some cases, all the above. If you look at the videos by the channel called *Roseology*, she uses all of it, including a meditation.

If you do a few of these and you don't hit the mark, you may want to take note if you were attracted to just the color of the crystal or the back of the deck design. Sometimes that's what tells you it's the one!

And other times it's your mind standing between you and your intuition. If you make notes of your experience, you'll be that much closer to being connected to your intuition, and you'll catch your mind trying to sneak in and run the show because that's the job of our mind.

Tune in Throughout the Day

You can tune into your intuition throughout the day. Your body is telling you things that override your mind all day long. You just don't recognize it as intuition. That's how natural it is. But today we stuff it down in favor of our monkey minds.

You're young, and we encourage you to tune into your body and observe the sensations while you work, talk to people, and walk around town. You'll grow into adulthood with a better radar than most people around you.

Intuitive Tarot Card Reading

Here we'll go over how to begin reading the cards intuitively. You'll also be able to put yourself on the spot in feeling the sensations you get with making intuitive choices and strengthen the daily tuning we just discussed.

Go to your quiet sacred space. Do the meditation and prepare yourself as prescribed in the first part of the guide. Begin by shuffling the cards. Just shuffle them for three to five minutes without a thought about anything you want to ask. We aren't asking questions in this exercise and we aren't doing spell work.

We're just tuning in and merging with the cards. Close your eyes and focus on the way they feel in your hands and the motion of how you personally choose to shuffle them.

Now, most of you may have already Googled how to shuffle cards or someone taught you. We want you to forget all of that and just let the cards move between both hands. They can be shuffled the way a card dealer fans them and then pushes them back together or they can be shuffled sideways; it doesn't matter, just make the shuffle your own.

If the way you were taught is your natural and most comfortable way to do it then by all means do so, but don't do it that way because you think it's the 'right' way.

Now, choose any card from the top of the deck. Look at it for a quick moment. Place it down and write in your journal what the card means to you with the very first glance. There is no wrong way to answer. If you're new to Tarot, then this should be no issue because you are just learning. Your mind hasn't learned to get in the way yet.

Next, pick up the card again and look at it for three minutes. Really look at the pictures. Look at the card as if you found it on the street and didn't know what it was, or you saw it in an art gallery and weren't aware it was a Tarot card. What does it tell you in the picture? What does it remind you of? What is it saying to you?

Write down your impressions. Now let the same card sit under your pillow. Sleep on it and in the morning while you're in a half-awake state, look at it. Lay there and just look at it. Then write down what you think.

It doesn't matter if the impressions are all different each time you look at the card at the beginning. It only matters that your mind is collecting the data you're giving it. Then, when you come across the card in a reading, BAM! You'll get something and it will be accurate!

We suggest starting with the Major Arcana. There are 22 cards, and we want you to spend a day on each. On the 23rd day, we want you to do a reading, a short one for yourself. Not a yes or no reading, but a short, one-card reading to give you some simple advice about something you don't know the answer to already.

Then, start incorporating the other cards one suit at a time. You'll see at the end of a three-month period you'll be a more intuitive reader than not!

Intuitive Reading Advanced Exercises

After you've done the cards intuitively one by one, and you've at least done the Major Arcana and one suit of the Minor Arcana, you can begin to pull a story together as you did with the book meanings—but now you'll do it intuitively.

Do the preparation as usual: get into a meditative state and perform the shuffling exercises. When you feel like they're done, take the Major Arcana and separate them from the other cards. Now, go back and shuffle the Major Arcana with a simple question that can be answered with two cards only. When you feel they're done shuffling, choose one Major Arcana card from the top of the deck.

Don't try and think it out or remember any meaning you may have associated with it from your practice. Just put it on the table and immediately pick up the Minor Arcana. Shuffle them in the same manner and choose one card from the top of the deck. Place it next to the first card.

Take your first instinct of the cards together. If you draw a blank or something comes to mind that you believe to be silly or inappropriate, it doesn't matter. Write out what you see and feel. You can't be wrong. This is your own interpretation, and it is always correct!

Now, look up the traditional meanings of the cards. Write down the main keywords of the book's meaning. You'll find one of two things. That your intuition matches a large percentage of the book's meaning and your intuitive meaning, or your meaning will be wildly off track from the book. Either way, it's correct. You are going to have a distinct signature; a pattern that is different because you are unique.

Now, Let's Formulate Some Questions

Let's go back to some question formulas. You'll use the same process you did previously in the last exercise. First write out what you instinctively see and then what the book says and compare. Also, we say "book" meanings, but don't be shy to look up other meanings.

The great thing about Tarot or any other esoteric niche is that things are always being discovered about how to use them, and many great teachers are out there with their own brand of interpretation and you are free to experiment and choose what you believe. Isn't that amazing!?

Question Formulation Exercise

Separate the Major Arcana and the court cards, and then keep the Minor Arcana together. Formulate the question in your mind for this exercise. Practice this exercise for each question and do this a few times a week until you're comfortable. Here's how you do it.

Steps:

Formulate questions that are simple and that include these elements:

1. A person, only one for now.
2. A theme, such as love, career, or finances.

Do the preparations as described in this guide and get centered at your altar or the sacred space where you perform your readings. Formulate any question you want with the above guide.

1. Shuffle the Major Arcana first and choose one card from the top when you feel you are done.
2. Do the same with the court cards and choose one. This is representing the person you have in mind involved in your question. The gender doesn't matter, it's the character and energy that you sense off the card.
3. Choose the next card from the deck of Minor Arcana.
4. Use the Intuitive Exercises you learned here.

After you've asked a few questions and gotten the hang of creating a story from the cards using both the book meaning and your intuition, you can add more cards and more shuffles.

Card Combinations

Here, we'll offer a way to discern the card combinations that you can use in reading interpretation and in spell work. We've made these quick and easy. You won't find an exhaustive listicle-style card combination sheet, but you will get the main and most important ways of figuring out what the cards are telling you when they're side by side. This is another type of exercise that's geared to intuitive development. It's all a habit.

Keep in mind that you don't need to separate the cards for this, nor do you need to know every combination because you are learning a concept.

All you need to know is to keep in mind the card meanings and the suits and what they represent. Then, you can apply your intuition or the book meaning—who cares, it's up to you!

Examples:

1. The Eight of Pentacles, which is working on building skills and apprenticeship with the High Priestess, will point to development of intuition or esoteric skills.

2. The Empress, which denotes fertility and ideas, with the Ten of Wands may mean too much mental overload and trying too hard for the things of the Empress; or the Queen of Swords can denote being sterile physically or devoid of ideas.
3. The Seven of Swords and the Nine of Wands. You're paranoid because you are engaging in unsavory acts. You fear being caught for something you've secretly done!
4. The Nine of Cups and the Nine of Pentacles. You've achieved your independence and now you've had your wishes fulfilled! You are satisfied alone, but not lonely.
5. The Seven of Cups and the Two of Pentacles. Wow, you're really burning the candle at both ends and juggling too much. This is because you're not making a solid choice and you're throwing good energy after bad!
6. The Strength card and the Two of Wands. Wait, be strong and an answer will soon come. Weigh out all of your possibilities and trust that the Universe will give you the sign to go ahead!
7. The Magician and the Tower, Death, or any card that denotes endings. This says you need to be careful not to try and force anything to stick around because the end of a cycle will bring better things.
8. The Magician and the Sun or Star, or any card that denotes new beginnings. This tells you that you are in the driver's seat and you should in fact be ready to manifest what you want as a good outcome is possible now!
9. Judgment and any court card denote being careful about the character of others. Someone's behavior needs to improve before you can go forward with them. If it doesn't, it's best to let them go!
10. The Fool and the Six of Cups denote a childlike attitude or reunion with a childhood friend or old romantic partner.

With these ten you should get the main point of how to put them together just based on the meaning alone. You'll get quicker and better at it as you practice. In the next section there is another quick guide to using the numerology of the cards to understand the cycles of a situation, so you know at what phase of a situation you are in.

Reading Cycles in the Tarot

A full cycle is 1-10. The cards are there for this purpose and are numbered in this way for you to see the cycles you are in so you can make educated decisions. You will also know better how long something may stick around by what the numbers say. Like the last section on combinations, you only need to know the concept and not every single possibility; and like the combinations, with practice, this will become second nature to you.

Examples:

The guide for the below examples is as follows:

Cards numbered: 1,2,3 are the beginning of a cycle.

Cards numbered: 4,5,6 are in the middle of a cycle.

Cards numbered: 7,8,9,10 are at the end of a cycle.

1. Ace of Cups and Eight of Cups. Relationships start but seem to end without the prospect of starting again as the relationship is not serving you.
2. Two of Wands and Seven of Pentacles. There is a partnership or a collaboration of ideas that are now gearing up to being put into practice.

You get the point. Let's practice together now.

Grab your deck and start shuffling. Phrase the question in the prescribed open-ended fashion. What will be so if_____? Fill in the blank with your own situation.

Pull two random cards. Intuit or read the book meaning, and then look at the numerology. Write down the result and see if it resonates or if it comes into being.

Important Note:

It's a good practice to date your journal when you do these readings because you'll be able to look back with greater clarity for accuracy.

Time to Advance!

Now, it's time to advance! Use ALL the exercises in the book and use PURE intuition! Ditch the book and go with what you feel. Cut loose, have fun, and let your hair down!

Symbolism and Intuition

Now, we will bring in another fun element to the mix, the symbolism. The cards will be interpreted further with no use of the book, and if you thought we were going to mention specific cards—you're wrong! Below are examples of what you are going to look for in each card to complete this section.

This is exciting! Possibly the most exciting part of the book!

Steps:

1. Do the cleansing preparation as prescribed in this book or use your own.
2. Sit at your sacred space and shuffle as described in this book or in your own way.
3. When you are ready, pull a card, any card. Place it in a playing card holder, in your hands, or anywhere that it will stand upright. These are only suggestions.
4. Look from the background of the image to the objects and scenery closest to you.

You may notice things like:

- Clouds or blue sky
- Structures like castles or homes
- The ground color and what it's made of—is it desert or dirt or something else?
- People and animals
- Otherworldly beings

Now, take a look at the climate and tone of these objects.

- Is the water in the card raging or calm?
- Is the sand blowing wildly or flat?

- What are the beings in the picture's mood like?
- Are they holding anything?
- Are the buildings and objects in good repair?
- Is the sky a depressed color?

Bring these elements together to tell a story in that one card. Write it down and let's move on.

Symbolism in Card Combinations

Now, we try and take the card combinations as we did in that section and look at what they may have in common. How is the Universe trying to speak to you in the symbolism in the cards?

- Are there any similarities in the two cards chosen?
- Look for things like angels, dark clouds, castles, etc.

What stands out to you the most? Now, put your meaning in the context of your question. Did you have an aha! moment? We'll bet you did, or you soon will with practice.

This concludes the section, and we hope you've had a lot of fun. We suggest returning back to the guide to get your practice in.

The next two sections will give you some correlations between the cards and other elements you can use. Lastly, we will go into the Tarot and Ancestral work and Guides and Beings. There is also an index with a few tried and true good books on more.

Tarot and Astrology

The Tarot and its symbolism have associations you won't see in the images of the cards necessarily. Today, there are many decks that highlight astrology and colors etc. and, just so you know, you'll find just as many interpretations. Our advice is to start with the guidance you have here and then intuitively discern what is best for you to follow.

In this part of the guide, we'll use the Major Arcana because they are the cards with the richest symbolism. You will use that same symbolism in all your rituals and for using the planets in your readings and your spells.

Tarot, Planetary, and Zodiac Correlations

1. Sun – The Sun
2. Moon – The Moon and High Priestess
3. Mercury – The Magician
4. Empress – Venus
5. Mars – The Tower
6. Jupiter – The Wheel of Fortune
7. Saturn – The World
8. Uranus – The Fool
9. Neptune – The Hanged Man
10. Pluto – Judgment

Since you've been such a diligent student and you've gotten all the way to this, near the end of the guide, we'll throw in a way to do a reading with Tarot and an astrology chart. It's not hard and you needn't know any astrology. We'll give you what you need right here!

The astrological houses and what they mean are below. Keep this handy with the planetary meanings above and we can move forward with your reading instruction.

1. First House – Self, ruled by Aries, Mars
2. Second House – Material Possessions, Security, Taurus
3. Third House – Community, Communication, Gemini, Mercury

4. Fourth House – Home, Family, Moon, Cancer
5. Fifth House – Romance, Creativity, Leo, Sun
6. Sixth House – Work, Routine, Health, Virgo, Mercury
7. Seventh House – Relationships, Contracts, Partners, Libra, Venus
8. Eighth House – Death, Sex, Inheritance, Mystery, Scorpio, Mars, Pluto
9. Nineth House – Travel, Philosophy, Jupiter, Sagittarius
10. Tenth House – Public Image, Career, Legacy, Capricorn, Saturn
11. Eleventh House – Community, Friends, Collaboration, Aquarius, Saturn, Uranus
12. Twelvth House Collective – Unconscious, Psychic Abilities, Pisces, Jupiter, Neptune

The next step is to use the chart below. This will give you even more insight into what the person or you may be going through. You may not get this anywhere else, at least not without asking someone who knows, but it works. You can print this chart out or look for a template online.

The houses are labeled 1 to 12 as they typically are. Take the template and mark each house starting with house 1 and mark it 13, then house 2 as 4, house 3 as 15, and so on. Continue around the chart until you get to around 80. That is the typical lifespan.

Each house will represent the experiences of a person at the ages that you've put in each house. So, for example, house 1 is 1 and also 13 and so on. You can use this in a reading to determine what a person is going through.

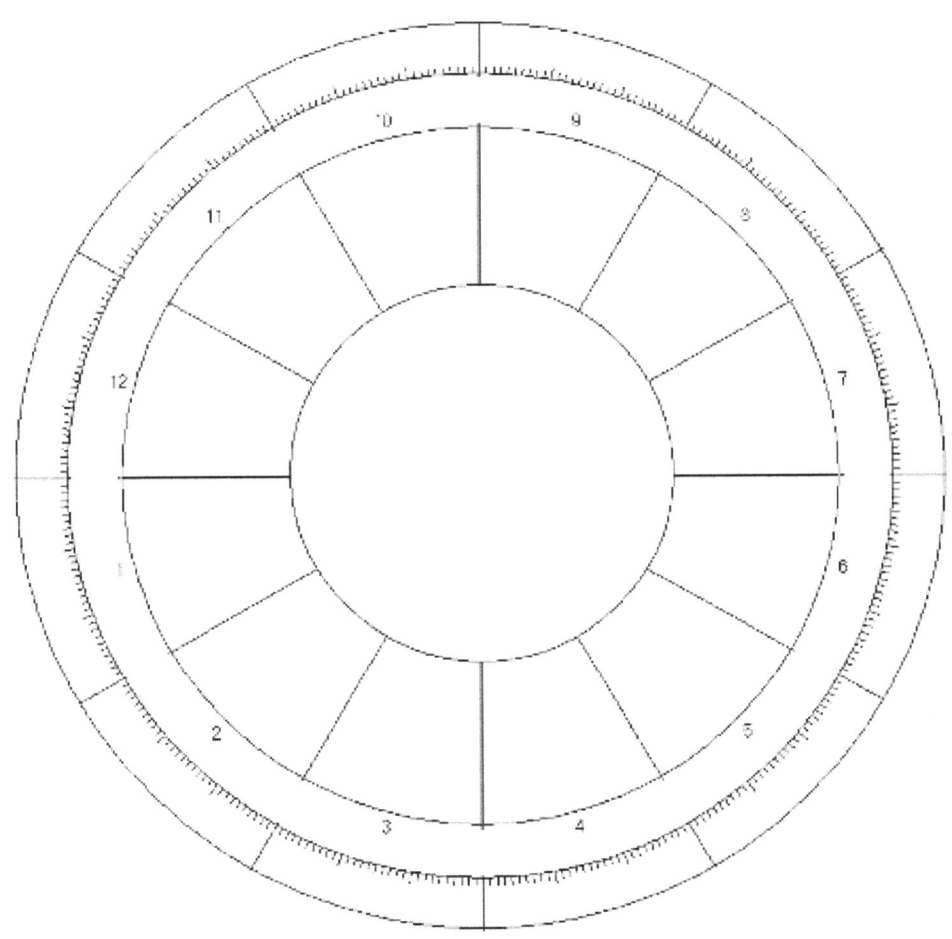

If you decide to read for others this process is a great backup for getting in touch with your client's life and you'll look like the youngest Tarot reading genius ever! It's what we want for you!

An Important Note:

When you are working with others, even friends, you'll get people more times than not that won't want to tell you anything. The attitude is largely that if you're the psychic then you should know.

At your stage in life, other kids will do this too— but have no fear, that's where you pull out the extra special sauce like this reading. You don't have to be told anything. What you know now about the cards and the chart will get you where you need to go on the right track.

Steps:

1. You already know how to prepare. If not, go back and look through the book again, but we have total confidence in you that you'll know what you're doing.
2. Shuffle the cards and get in tune.
3. Pull the cards and place them in whatever reading you are doing.
4. Start with your immediate intuition of course, then the numbers and the symbolism. Get in touch with the overarching symbolism first. Are there a lot of dark or bright cards? Where are they in the cycles of life? How do the numbers correlate to the part of life the card represents? For example, the Ace of Cups may indicate the start of a new relationship, and then the Death card with the Ten of Pentacles indicates a divorce or job loss, etc. This is where you get an overall view.
5. Before you say a word, look at the planetary rulership of the Major Arcana you have there. Now, what are the houses they rule? This is also a great indicator of the situations they may be finding themselves in. Look at the card positions to see if it's already happened in the past or coming up in the future.
6. Then finally, look at the chart to compare their age to the wheel and house.

From here, you should have as thorough a snapshot as you could possibly have, and any unclear messages can be clarified with clarifier cards.

Whew! That was your most advanced reading, but we promise you, you'll be on top of it on automatic in no time!

PART 6: BRINGING IN THE BEINGS AND KEEPING IT ALL IN THE FAMILY

Congratulations on making it this far! You are young, bright, and very devoted. This is the most important quality to making a master Tarot reader! You are well on your way to becoming the Jedi; a person armed with the wisdom of the ages.

We trust that you have practiced and know how to do the main takeaways of this book. Look at the list quickly before beginning the last part of the book about beings and ancestor work. Please go back over the stuff you aren't sure of, as well as the protection ritual, because your world is about to become more magnificent, and we want you well prepared!

Do You Understand and Are You Comfortable With?

- How to protect yourself and your sacred space?
- The myths about Tarot so that you are confident?
- How to phrase a question and your emotional state?

Bringing in the Beings

At some point during your reading and ritual practices you may start to notice that synchronicity and signs start to get noticed. This is happening because your crown chakra, which we will go into briefly later, is opening and so is your third eye chakra located between your eyebrows. Once you begin to open yourself to the higher realms it's important to stay connected to the Divine and THEN, to your own spirit guides.

The reason why we say the Divine first is that this is the creator force of which you are a part. We all are, we just tend to forget. This is the most powerful protective force there is and will dominate anything or anyone else coming through.

Once you begin to feel that what we lovingly call your spirit team connecting with you, you'll want to be sure not to fear anything. Remember your emotional state will dictate what forces you bring in.

Most of what we like to call 'bad forces' are just an out-of-balance form of ourselves and our shadow side. We touched on that. That's the inner shadow you collect over time, that at your age may not be a thing, but we need to be sure to understand we are protected.

If you have any doubts, which is completely normal, call upon the Divine in whatever form you believe. Have a white candle and protective objects on your altar. You can even just call it the Divine or source. The important thing is you FEEL protected should there be a doubt.

You'll want to create a relationship with that force, and then you can start to work with your spirit team who can talk through the cards. In fact, it's the easiest way to get to most people since seeing and hearing them are a bit difficult for most people, but the cards make it much easier!

Important Facts About Your Spirit Guides

The first important fact about spirit guides is that they can be anyone. They can be parts of your higher self, which is you in higher form. They can be ancestors, angels, Star people, and passed loved ones.

It's important for you to know how to tell the difference between all of them. When you read Tarot for yourself or others, you want the clearest, highest, most unbiased answer.

You wouldn't think that your spirit guides would give you anything but that; however, they can. They have personalities and beliefs just like incarnated humans do and will guide you according to them. How do we know? The same way you'll learn to understand the connection. Through years of practice and interaction.

You May Want to Go Way Back in the Ancestral Chain

Your ancestors are everyone from your immediate family to the beginning of your ancestral lineage. They seem to have a large stake in our lives as they watch us do our thing. The closest ones, whether you knew them or not, will be the last three generations from your parents. So, grandparents, great grandparents, and so forth. When we ask them for help or to guide us in some way, we're essentially giving someone with a lot of bias a one-way ticket to take the wheel. This may not be for your best and highest good, but they'll mean well.

Let's look at an example.

You're doing a Tarot reading on a relationship you are having. You feel they're a great fit for you, but mom doesn't and because she or dad may not, your long-passed nanny may hate the person for you. What kind of advice do you think you'll get?

You don't want to look at the breakup or even cards that tell you they're cheating and dump the poor person. And yes, word to the wise, just as any human being can twist the truth or outright lie, so can spirit guide ancestors.

Not always because they're bad people, but because they want what they feel is best for you. Maybe they've been working behind the scenes to bring someone else in.

So, what do you do in this case? You set the intention that the Divine only filters through the messages for your highest good. Period. Done in faith, without guilt or shame, this works like a charm.

How to Best Work with Tarot and Your Ancestors, Angels, Star Beings

Ancestral Work

This takes a bit of research, but it's fun and will teach you a lot about your lineage. A lot of us have karmic contracts and unhealthy patterns that need to be broken and that's the reason your ancestors are hanging around your Tarot altar waiting for you to say Hi!

You can start with your parents. Ask them questions about your lineage. If they don't know much, then Ancenstry.com and other resources we will have at the end of this book in the suggested reading and resources section will help you.

Get a firm enough grip on your nationality and where your family line on both mom and dad's side came from. So, if they were African or Guianese or Irish, you could create a separate space on your Tarot altar with some representational artifacts that would draw them.

Another protective gesture is to have offerings. What is the flower or the food of the region they come from? Place it there along with pictures of any ancestors you have.

If your roots are deep into the island regions and Africa, there is a plethora of information about those cultures with instructions on what those tribes loved. Then you can connect with their energy and you'll know after a while that it's them talking through the cards and not someone else!

Always make sure you respect them and never shout, curse, or get mad at them in any way. If there's something you don't like, you have free will to change it.

Angelic Realms

The angelic realms seem to have become quite a fashion since the 1980s and there's much information out there about them. What you can do to be sure you are speaking to the right beings, such as the more popular ones like Archangel Michael and Metatron, is find the true seals to each of them. These are the sigils that vibrate with the correct name of the correct angel. This way, when asking a question or asking for protection, you'll get used to the right intuitive feeling and know it's them.

Oracle Cards

Angel Oracles are one of the best ways as a beginner or even seasoned Tarot reader to begin to communicate with the Angelic realms. They have the names of the angels and what they represent already there on the cards so you can't really go wrong.

This is also a great way to invite them and or what they represent to connect with you during a reading or meditation if you are uncomfortable in evoking them to join you.

Doreen Virtue placed a lot of herself in the Angel Oracle cards she developed for decades and became the inventor of the first real angel oracles in fact. Just a word of warning, she is now Christian and no longer really deals in the metaphysical, but we suggest you give some of her stuff we have in the resource section a shot.

As you sprout into adulthood or even before, you'll get to know the ever-changing landscape of the spiritual community. We must honor all paths as we would want others to do so for us.

Star Beings

These beings are the most elusive because there's so much information about them and the different factions that have been channeled by people, we can easily get confused; but we think we should cover this also in brief because it's something you may run into once you are working on the spiritual plane.

Star beings, according to intel, are multidimensional and part of the 4th, 5th, and any of the many timelines we have. So best you know how to deal with them and recognize when they're communicating to you.

Galactic Oracle Cards

You get lucky with the galactic spiritual team the same way you do the Angelic realm. Mystics that have come before you have developed Oracle cards that are geared toward all of the star tribes, we think we know of today. You can also do your own research on them and find out what each of them may want to convey through the Tarot and Oracle.

Most Popular Galactic Teams you'll find in Tarot Oracles are:

- Pleiades
- Arcturians
- Sirius
- Arghathian
- Apex
- Orion

At this point you have all the protection and the know-how to really learn the cards to an extent of mastery from beginner to advance with practice. The next section will give you resources and quick guides to finding more reading and information.

Quick Guide to Chakras and the Tarot

We thought we'd include this because you can find chakra decks to integrate with the Tarot as you get more comfortable, just as you will the Angels and Galactic team Oracles. You should also know what chakras are activated when you read cards and start to open up more to the realm of spirit.

The crown is above the head and the third eye is on the forehead between the eyes. These are the first chakras to open when awakening to the realm of spirit. The High Priestess and the Fool are, in our opinion, represented by those chakras.

The Throat Chakra can be akin to any card that represents communication and speech, air dominant cards.

The Heart Chakra represents the Cups or water dominant cards.

The Solar Plexus Chakra represents the Sun and any fire dominant cards. Remember we said they were interchangeable with air in some decks—Wands here for the sake of this guide.

The Sacral Chakra between the hip bones and below the navel is represented also by the Cups and water, but as you get more comfortable with your intuition you can interchange that one between fire and water since it's creation as well as emotion.

The Root Chakra is at the base of the spine and is our security; any material and money cards and the suit of Pentacles can be represented here.

If you want to know where the blocks are to success, health, love, etc., throw one card at a time until you are comfortable that all the imbalanced chakras have been accounted for. This is a little advanced but there are Oracle cards with chakras on them that you can use with the Tarot as well.

After a while, the trick we taught you about viewing the pictures on the cards will begin to pop right out at you.

For example, you throw a card with the intention of getting a read on the chakra system or even your own; it doesn't matter, just don't go diagnosing health issues—that's never good, not just on cards. Look at the card the way we showed you, and take note of what you notice. The Sacral Chakra is orange colored so if you get cards with that color you are getting a message. Then, look at the meaning or intuit in it if you're ready to do that, and look at the tone of the card. This should tell the story.

Below are the chakra colors:

1. Crown: Purple
2. Third Eye: Indigo Blue
3. Throat: Cobalt or any Blue
4. Heart: Pink or Green
5. Solar: Yellow or Gold
6. Sacral: Orange
7. Base: Red

Chakra Reading Meditation

Steps:

1. Sit or your client sits and takes some mindful breaths.
2. When relaxed, you or they will shuffle the cards in any fashion comfortable.
3. As you or they shuffle slowly and mindfully, you or they imagine a golden and diamond white light coming slowly from the ground up to the Base Chakra; hold it for about 30 slow seconds and repeat with each chakra.
4. Maintain shuffling the entire time. The whole process takes no more than two to three minutes.
5. You or they pull a card from the top, bottom, or middle of the deck. It doesn't matter—wherever you or they feel it.

BAM! That is the chakra that represents the issues at hand and needs work.

6. Take that card and place it in the middle of the table and do your reading for whatever they or you want to know, or just a general reading or one centered around the chakra. It doesn't matter. The reading may show other secondary chakras that need some help.

You can couple this with the astrology chart technique or any number of the things we taught you here.

Resources and Further Reading and Information

This section has some resources to take you further into your Tarot and spiritual journey. We hope that you'll continue to visit us for more up-to-date information and training.

Before we get into the tools, we would like to cover how to choose your decks and other tools you may use on your spiritual journey. We would also like to guide you on how to clean these things because for a beginner, we feel you need to have a ritual until you are comfortable; then all you really need is white, gold, or violet light protection that comes from visualization.

The only purpose of a ritual is to make the mindset and energy of the person performing it more powerful. In the case of reading Tarot cards, it's a matter of clearing energies from others and even when reading for yourself, clearing energies from between your own readings.

Why is this important? Whether you are reading for yourself or not, you are creating an emotional vibration and that vibration is what is telling the cards to work for you.

So, it's already infused with your vibe from the last question. Same thing goes for reading for others. Their energy may transfer from one person's reading to another. This means someone is not getting the proper answer and this needs to be addressed.

Sage and incense sets can easily be found on Amazon, or any others you find will do well if you can't make noise where you are or at the time of the reading, and you can't use bells or singing bowls.

Steps to Cleansing Cards and Choosing Decks

After you are finished asking one question or reading for one person and are expecting another client, you should first start by shuffling with the intention to clear the cards from the intention of the reading.

Next, light some white sage or black sage if the emotion was negative or heavy in any way. In an anti/counterclockwise circle, wave the incense over the cards, set it down on a fireproof tray (get parents' permission by the way) and allow the smoke to go through the cards as you shuffle them.

Walk around your space in the same anti/counterclockwise position and clear it.

Choosing your Deck

When choosing a deck, it needs to call to you. Even if you are purchasing one we suggested, or you look for yourself. Sit in front of the screen and take your time to look at them slowly. Browse with as empty a head as you can. Use your intuition without reading the description or reviews or anything as of yet.

The one that pulls you is the one you investigate. Now, if your parents or you gave you a budget, then of course look with the intention of staying within that budget. You can't make a wrong choice. Don't worry if it's not a beginner's deck. If one really pulls at you then get it. There's a resonance there that we suggest you follow.

www.ingramcontent.com/pod-product-compliance
Lightning Source LLC
Chambersburg PA
CBHW081345070526
44578CB00005B/733